To John & Jean —
I'm glad we've converted
some Padre fans to Ti
fans — may you too always fee[l]
Safe At Home

Shawn
Teegens
Joshua 24:15

To John & Jean
Best Wishes
Mike Hargrove

Safe at Home

Sharon Hargrove
and
Richard Hauer Costa

Safe at Home

A Baseball Wife's Story

TEXAS A&M
UNIVERSITY
PRESS
College
Station

Frontispiece:
Mike and Sharon Hargrove

The paper used in this book
meets the minimum requirements
of the American National Standard
for Permanence of Paper
for Printed Library Materials,
Z39.48-1984.
Binding materials
have been chosen
for durability.

Library of Congress Cataloging-in-Publication Data
Hargrove, Sharon, 1951–
    Safe at home : a baseball wife's story / Sharon Hargrove and
Richard Hauer Costa. — 1st ed.
        p. cm.
    Includes index.
    ISBN 0-89096-376-2 (alk. paper)
    1. Hargrove, Mike.   2. Baseball players—United States.
3. Hargrove, Sharon, 1951–   . 4. Baseball players' wives—United
States—Biography.   I. Costa, Richard Hauer.   II. Title.
GV865.H25H37   1989
796.357'092'4—dcB   —dc19   88-31594
                                                                CIP

To Mike, who said the words "I love you" and
   then taught me their meaning;
to our four kids, in hopes that this book will
   help them see that their sacrifices have
   been worthwhile;
to my mom, whose positive outlook on life
   prepared me for a life in baseball;
to the memory of my late dad and to my
   brothers, Al and Ben, whose love of sports
   infected me early on;
to my grandmother Gee Gee, who encour-
   aged me to write this book.

To Philip Costa, for having been the amiable
   sharer of his dad's obsession for baseball
   and the first reader of this book.

And to baseball.

Contents

Preface
Why Sharon and I Wrote This Book

JUST about the only thing folks on the outside know about baseball wives is what the TV camera picks out, scanning the choice family boxes they occupy, all of them dolled up as if they had just stepped out of a bandbox. But in the boonies, where the lighting is poor and only some 100-watt radio station ever mentions them, they can wear blue jeans and worry about the rent.

For nearly twenty years—and still counting—Sharon and Mike Hargrove have been growing up with baseball. In the summer of 1987, when we began this book, they were in the Carolina League (Class A). Mike was managing the Kinston, North Carolina, Indians for Cleveland, the team he had finished up with in 1985 after twelve years as a first baseman/outfielder in the major leagues. With Mike, who was thirty-seven, were the members of the Hargrove family: his wife, Sharon, thirty-six, their three girls, Kim, twelve, Missy, ten, Pam, eight, and the "baby," Andy, five.

Kinston—population just under twenty-five thousand—was the Hargroves' seventeenth stop, counting rookie instructional leagues and spring training (as player, coach, and manager), among both the citrus and the cactus. Sharon estimates that she and Mike have made fifty-seven moves since their marriage in 1970. For all these years, wherever Mike went, Sharon and the kids went, too. That is part of the reason why we wrote this book.

If you've been an avid ball fan since the mid-1970s, you'll remember Mike Hargrove. He played five seasons with the Texas Rangers (1974–78), mostly as a first baseman, although he also played the outfield and was designated hitter. You may also remember that Mike had a ritual as a batter that slowed the games somewhat. Early in his Cleveland years (1979–85), a Toronto sportswriter dubbed Hargrove the "Only Human Rain Delay."

Still, he must have been doing something right. He hit .290 lifetime, which must put him up around the ninety-ninth percentile among hitters all-time. I knew about Mike Hargrove. He was always, as they say in baseball, a "tough out." Invariably, when I was at Arlington Stadium watching, he would be in the middle of the Rangers' game-winning rallies against my favorites, the Oakland Athletics.

A lot of years have gone by since the Saturday in early April, 1974, when twenty-three-year-old Sharon (Rupprecht) Hargrove of Perryton, Texas, presented herself in the wives' section as Mrs. Dudley Michael Hargrove, the wife of the Rangers' rookie first baseman. Manager Billy Martin didn't play Mike in that home season–opening game against the world champion A's. It proved one of the last games Mike wouldn't start that year.

Sharon and I met in the summer of 1986 in the stands in the Upper Mohawk Valley city of Little Falls, New York, where the hometown Mets were hosting the Batavia Trojans. Recently retired Texas A&M coach Tom Chandler, a close friend of mine, was managing the Batavia team for the Cleveland Indians. My wife and I, for the fourth straight summer, had fled Texas for Upstate New York as soon as A&M's first summer session ended. Tom and I had arranged for a reunion as soon as his team's schedule brought him either to Little Falls or to Utica, both cities a short drive from our cottage on Oneida Lake at Sylvan Beach. On Monday evening, August 4, the Trojans were to play a night game with the Mets. After we had exchanged greetings, Tom said; "You won't believe who my hitting coach is—*Mike Hargrove!*"

And there he was, hitting fungoes to the Batavia fielders from the lefty side. Once the game started, Tom and Mike suggested I might enjoy sitting with the five other Hargroves. Mike and Sharon had been upstate once before—his first professional season in 1972. He, like Pete Rose (I would later discover), had broken in with the Geneva team of the New York–Penn League, although Rose arrived twelve years before Mike. In the summer of 1986, with their four kids in tow, the Hargroves had revisited Niagara Falls and were planning their first visit to the Baseball Hall of Fame museum at nearby Cooperstown.

I remember Sharon as a central figure in a tableau that has remained with me from the start: Sharon, blonde and piquant, chatting with a fan while dispensing popcorn to Andy; Kim, the oldest, the large official score book in her lap, writing down the lineups; Missy and Pam, flitting from tier to tier as the stands began filling.

I don't remember who won that first game we saw together. I hardly watched the game. What I do recall was the good baseball talk with a woman who knew things about the game I had never much thought about.

I have no idea what her youngsters thought of the grandfatherly man who was distracting their mother's attention. A habit learned from fifteen years on newspapers before I became a college English teacher has always been to treat an interesting new acquaintance like an interviewee. As such, Sharon was certainly one of the best ever. Our rapport was instant, our talk, nonstop.

I should describe Sharon briefly. Think of a living refutation of what Dorothy Parker said about girls who wear glasses—that's Sharon. Think of the prettiest cheerleader you remember from high school or college — that's Sharon. I read somewhere that blondes have more fun. I have never known a time — and I was with her during at least two of those fifty-seven moves, none of which could have been other than enervating — when she wasn't enjoying herself and wanting everyone with her to enjoy.

Her features are cameo perfect in a way that is distracting only because you like to look at them. And she's a West Texan from the Panhandle. That means she'll occasionally say she "might could" do something or invent syntax that no English teacher could possibly diagram.

Much more important: she's a talker who also listens.

I, of course, took only mental notes during our first conversation. I remember one vivid commentary for whose exact wording I do not vouch but for whose sense I do. She was talking about baseball wife Danielle Torrez's then-recent book about her broken marriage to pitcher Mike Torrez, which she blamed on baseball fame. Sharon spoke of the divorced wife of a friend and former teammate of Mike's who kept going to court every time the former husband signed a new contract.

"Why doesn't she let him alone?" Sharon quoted Mike.

"Mike," Sharon quoted herself, "if you ever want out of our marriage because of one of those groupies, I'm just not about to make it easy. If it ever happens, just you tell that slut puppy that the four kids go with the deal. After she's pooped out from the kids, call me up and I'll show you a better time than she ever did!"

To this recital, Sharon quickly added, "It was all hypothetical — just bluffing. I would never give up our kids. Mike never even remotely called my bluff just as I never called his when he offered during his Rookie-of-the-Year season to quit ball if I was unhappy."

Driving back to Sylvan Beach, I couldn't get out of my mind something Sharon had said almost as an aside. "I've been making some notes for a book about our life in ball, but it's not getting off the ground." That night I wrote her a long letter, which I mailed to the Batavia address she had given me. I said I, too, had always wanted to write a book about baseball. Maybe I could do mine by helping her do hers.

Two weeks later, when Batavia was in Utica for a series with the Blue Sox, Sharon and Mike, accompanied by Tom Chandler, drove thirty-eight miles on the New York State Thruway to our cottage. That afternoon the writing of this book began.

Even though the Hargroves and the Costas both returned to Texas after the season, Perryton and College Station might as well have been on opposite coasts. We have had three working reunions. I visited Sharon in Perryton just before Thanksgiving, 1986. She came down to College Station during A&M's spring break the following year. In mid-August we blocked out the book in Kinston.

I've been reading *Five O'Clock Comes Early* (1982), the fine book former sports columnist George Vecsey wrote with pitcher Bob Welch on the latter's battle with alcoholism. Vecsey, noting the thousands of hours he spent taping with Welch across a table, said he couldn't have done the book without the indelible impressions he formed during a week's visit to the rehab facility where the pitcher began his recovery. My experience was similar to Vecsey's. Watching Sharon and Mike on the field and—more importantly —off, the four kids around them, was indispensable.

Why did we write this book? Baseball lovers are always complaining that too much of the game is played off the field—the strikes, the drugs, free agency, the million-dollar negotiations and renegotiations, the greed. There's another part of baseball that is lived off the field but is as integral to the game as a home run or a strikeout: the domestic side, the on-the-road side, the kids' side, the wives' side. Nobody is telling that story; we have tried.

—Dick Costa

Safe at Home

Introduction
Baseball Wifehood

You married? Well, didja scout your wife? I hope to hell you did because any guy gets married better scout that woman—whether she's gonna be hard to get along with or go operatin' around on him, or whether she's got potential as a partner or a mother.
— *Old baseball scout, quoted by Kevin Kerrane*

WHEN I married my junior high school sweetheart in 1970, little did I know this small-town Texan would drive me all over the United States as a baseball wife.

Being the wife of a professional baseball player isn't always what it's cracked up to be. I learned early on that a sense of humor is not only helpful but necessary. I have also learned to laugh when I'd have rather thrown my arms into the air screaming: "I give up, take me home!" But by then I'd forgotten where home was.

In Kevin Kerrane's book *Dollar Sign on the Muscle: The World of Baseball Scouting* (Avon, 1985), I read about ten criteria by which scouts judge a player: stamina/durability, anticipation, hustle, reflexes, poise, baserunning, size, coordination/agility, instinct, eyesight. A wife in baseball is judged by these criteria too, and, in a sense, her chances of making good as a wife of summer can be predicted on their bases.

Through our years in the game, I've seen wives literally make or break their husbands' careers. Even though the wisdom of the old scout just quoted applies to wives anywhere, it is especially applicable to this game. It is not for faint-hearted, uncommitted, inflexible powder puffs.

What does it take?

In the pages that follow I hold up for examination actual baseball situations and apply Kerrane's criteria to them. By so doing I am speculating on the patterns of the successful baseball wife versus the pitfalls of the unsuccessful.

Stamina/Durability

Successful: If you could survive at least two or three moves a year.

Unsuccessful: If you would complain about husband's constantly phoning late at night from a place where disco music is heard in background.

Anticipation

Successful: You have learned to take the phone off the hook at mealtimes and early morning to avoid intrusions on your time-outs from baseball.

Unsuccessful: You know you would have no trouble booing with the crowd when husband strikes out, thereby escaping recognition as his spouse.

Hustle

Successful: You can make fast exit to minimize embarrassment after one of your kids has set off emergency exit alarm at airport.

Unsuccessful: You are unable to juggle six complimentary tickets among ten relatives/friends.

Introduction

Reflexes

Successful: You can always bump husband's arm just as he is about to sign good-looking female fan's program.

Unsuccessful: You show surprise every time a baseball wife you knew with another team appears to have different hair color, cleavage, or other features from those you remember.

Poise

Successful: You are able to react gracefully when someone asks you if you are your husband's mother.

Unsuccessful: You are unable to step between mother-in-law and husband's manager when she complains she came one thousand miles to see her son who's not in the lineup.

Base Running

Successful: You show quickness in maneuvering husband, who is battling for a spot on the roster, out of place where jukebox is playing "Please Release Me."

Unsuccessful: You don't move quickly enough to have cable TV and VCR hooked up properly by the time husband returns from first road trip.

Size

Successful: You always leave enough room in the van to pack a porta-potty on cross-country trips.

Unsuccessful: You scratch up family car again because you assumed you could squeeze it into half a parking slot at stadium.

Coordination/Agility

Successful: You can contain yourself at Mass when bell is rung and your child yells "Charge!".

Unsuccessful: You can't discriminate between babies and luggage on airport carousel and frequently fail to grab both before departing.

Instinct

Successful: You invariably look relaxed at game when camera light goes on although four kids are driving you up the wall.

Unsuccessful: You always seem to have a mouthful of food when on camera (not to mention mustard on chin and blouse).

Eyesight

Successful: You have good enough peripheral vision to clip coupons while riding first class while nobody's looking.

Unsuccessful: You not only spot your husband's manager's new hairpiece but you compliment him on it.

Once you have passed the scouting report, you are ready for your vocabulary quiz. You will have mastered diamond patter once you learn that:

—an *athletic supporter* is not an avid sports fan but a jock strap;

—the *Big Show* is not a Broadway hit but the players' name for the major leagues;

—*delivery* does not refer to takeout pizza brought in while your husband is on the road but a pitcher's style;

—that *dig in* is not what your kids do at mealtime but what the batter does to ready himself at the plate;

—that *double* is not coupon day for twice the value but a two-base hit;

—that a *front runner* is not the run down the front of your panty hose but a fan who supports first-place teams only;

Introduction

—that *hit and run* is not what your kids do all day but a play where the batter hits while the baserunner is on the move;

—that a *hot dog* is not a tasty treat at the game but a player who shows off;

—that *pepper* is not a condiment but a pregame drill to test reflexes;

—that *ribbies* are not meat you toss on the grill but runs-batted-in;

—that a *tater* is not a veggie but a homerun;

—that a *sacrifice* is not foregoing the pleasure of a road trip but a play ordered by the manager in which batter gives self up to advance baserunner.

—that a *warmup* is not a fleece jogging suit but a pitcher preparing for the game;

—that the *yard* is not where you send your kids to play but your husband's name for the ballpark.

And that's baseball!

Panhandle Daze

T H I S book should have been called *We Grew Up in Baseball*, but somebody else took that for their book already or came mighty close. It's the truth, though. Of course, some things would have been the same without baseball. I would still be Mrs. Dudley Michael Hargrove of Perryton, Texas. I imagine we'd still have the four kids. Surest of all is that I'd have spent all of my years in Perryton or some other Panhandle town.

It would have been Perryton with a difference, however. We wouldn't be living on six acres five miles straight east of Main Street, where every clear night we can watch the sun slipping below the horizon and see in silhouette our biggest grain elevator.

We have seen most of the country by now, but looking to the west—to Perryton—in the evening is our slice of Americana.

I'll be saying it over and over, one way or another. If you hook on with a professional baseball player, you're going to be driving past a lot of trucks with your U-Haul behind you or, with all your kids, riding practically standing up in one of those big vans Mike and I started buying after successive trades from Texas to San Diego to Cleveland had us covering 10,000 miles in just seven months.

We always come back to Perryton before, during, and after the season.

Since 1982 Mike and I can say with accuracy, "Meanwhile back at the ranch." We can't say our six acres are the House That Babe Ruth Built, but we can say it's the spread that baseball made not only possible but necessary. To be sure, there's gold in baseball, but there's a goldfish-bowl side, too. After the eight-month annual exposure, warts and all, it's good to get back to our own private domain. To borrow the title of a show on public radio, our place is our "Prairie Home Companion." Nothing for miles and miles in any direction but one grain elevator, two wheat fields, and, in better times, several productive oil wells. The three main economies of the Panhandle and West Texas, generally, press in on us if we care to look at them. What really presses in, though, are the tumbleweeds. No matter how many times Mike goes out with the pickup to pick those tumbleweeds off our fences, there will be a new batch in a half-hour.

There was a time — a brief time, thank goodness — when we were paying on three spreads — one in each of the three cities where Mike played ball. It was not so much that we were so well off as it was the nature of pro ball. We have always bought wherever we've been for longer than a cup of coffee. To some people, owning a house on the lake in Arlington, Texas, a condominium in San Diego, and a split-level near Cleveland is either showboating or really living high on the hog. It's neither. Having a place to set ourselves down is what it's all about. But we were not building castles at any of those places. Not even on our six acres.

If we had ever got to thinking of any of our big places as castles, we probably couldn't have lived in a college dorm the way we did in Batavia, New York, in 1986, or in a two-bedroom apartment, like we did during summer, 1987, at Kinston, North Carolina.

Sure, we got accustomed to life in the Big Show, but we know all about life in the boonies, too. During the sum-

mers of 1986 and 1987, we retraced in coaching and managing
—nonplaying roles—the same steps we took on the field.
We knew then—and we are learning again—that life's a
162-game schedule and some years you'll be out of the race
by July. Baseball's a street where you keep seeing the same
potholes. And they are not all in the low minors, either.
Even when we hit the right combination, we never took
it for granted the numbers wouldn't change.

Change. I read something in a textbook once about
change, and I think it applies to us. The more you think
things are changing the more you end up knowing they are
the same. That's Mike and me. Mike's a farm kid from
Texas, and he has resisted changing so far. You can't talk
with me a minute, in season or out, without knowing I'm
small-town West Texas from the Panhandle.

Like I said, ball has helped us grow up, but it has let us
stay the same, too. There's something about being Texans
—small-town Texans—that stays solid even in an unreal
world, which is what baseball is. Knowing about our hometown explains a lot of it.

At the turn of the century most communities in the
Texas Panhandle spent years in developing into incorpo-
rated cities and towns. In contrast, Perryton formed practically overnight with the merging of the communities of
Gray, Oklahoma, and Old Ochiltree, Texas. That was in
1889. Local histories will tell you these two merged into
Perryton to reap the benefits of the railroad that went between Gray and Old Ochiltree. No doubt about that. Still,
I like to think these settlers hated the very idea of com-
muting.

You take my grandparents on my mom's side (nobody has
to tell me there's nothing more tedious than listening to
someone else's genealogy; I promise to spare you all but
Grandma Gee Gee and Grandpa Jack). Kathryn (Gee Gee)
Allen, who is A.O.K. at eighty-six (that's *a*lert *o*pionionated
*k*ritter), came here from Albany, Texas, by a lucky accident

in the early 1920s. She had answered an ad for a teacher but missed a train connection—and the job, too. She found herself in Perryton. They needed a teacher also. She took the job and never did go back to Albany.

Grandma's husband was 84th District Judge Jack Rice Allen. Granddad was the first boy ever to graduate from Ochiltree High School, one of the earliest graduates of the University of Texas law school, and an early member of the Texas Bar. That was in 1916. He and Grandma were married in 1923. Granddad practiced law as soon as he returned from France after World War I. He held his judgeship from 1939 to 1957, at which time the 84th District lost its judge and I lost a lot more.

I was in the first grade when he died, but I'll never forget him. I think I inherited my outspokenness from Grandma Gee Gee. I know I inherited my need to keep our large family intact, come hell, highwater, or baseball, from Granddad.

It's hard for me to imagine how anybody, regardless of how much traveling they do, can lose their roots. Our kids have them though we've moved about almost constantly, from spring training through the long season into rookie Instructional League and more often than not, especially lately, in different places every year.

That's why it's always a good feeling to pull into our driveway off the state highway out of Amarillo.

Being Texans, Mike and I found his first five years in the Big Show especially gratifying. They were spent with the Texas Rangers. We always had this fantasy of a magic carpet —about four hundred miles of it—between the Panhandle and Dallas–Fort Worth, which would keep Perrytoners— our people—coming to Ranger games and us heading up there whenever we could.

I'm pretty sure, you see, that Mike was the first native Texan actually to put his John Henry to a Ranger contract. That was in 1972, the year the Washington Senators moved to Texas. (These were not the *old* Washington Senators. That franchise had moved to Minnesota. The team the Rangers replaced in 1972 had been reincarnated as the Washington Senators a few years earlier.) Mike's contract, of course, was not with the major league team just then. Texas Ranger scout Lee Anthony signed him for a short season at Geneva, New York, in lower Class A.

There was a left-handed pitching phenom named David Eugene Clyde who was signed by the Rangers' original owner, Bob Short. He came right out of a suburban Houston high school to the Big Show. David Clyde was the Rangers' first pick in the June, 1973, draft. According to Whitey Herzog in *The White Rat* (1987, p. 27), David was brought up prematurely to save a dying Texas franchise. I'd be less than honest if I didn't admit that Mike and I hoped Mike might exploit David's image and be brought up to the major leagues as a native son. When, after only two years in Class A, Mike survived Billy Martin's final cut to become Texas' regular first baseman, we just assumed we would play our whole career in Texas. Hadn't Mike been a Ranger in high school (Perryton Rangers) and in college (Northwestern State College Rangers)?

It just wasn't to be. When the Texas Rangers traded Mike after five seasons (three of them where he hit .300 or better), we thought we wouldn't survive.

You just say the word and it all comes back. My "sense of Yuma" is no joke. Yuma, just over the California border into Arizona and a desert community, is where the San Diego Padres still hold spring training. The one spring with the Padres and two months into the 1979 season in San Diego almost did Mike in. It was like we had been asked to sever our Texas roots. Mike and I never wanted him to leave the Texas womb.

Growing up in Perryton, we just never thought of leaving our hometown any more than Mike ever thought of leaving the Rangers. To stay in the region somewhere—a high school coaching family—was my dream, and I don't think Mike would have minded. I love words like *coach* and now—after our summer in Kinston—*manager*. They have the right sound. Believe me, Mike and I would have been nothing like the football coach and his wife in *The Last Picture Show*.

You've heard about high school football being a religion in Texas. You take a couple of kids from any of these oil and cattle towns in the Panhandle—places like Spearman, Hereford, Childress, Dalhart, Dumas—and you can bet that playing and watching sports will be a way of life. You can get into a conversation with anybody at the local drugstore and before you know it, you're talking football. Everybody's an armchair quarterback.

Mike Hargrove was our official quarterback.

Each year, in Childress, there's a Greenbelt Bowl football classic pitting the best of the Panhandle high school seniors—East versus West. In 1967, the guy I had been crazy about since seventh grade was selected quarterback, representing Perryton High. Our 1967 team went 9–1, and our quarterback, punter, extra-point kicker, and defensive back were all one guy, my steady, Mike Hargrove. (To give you an idea of how large a territory these Greenbelt teams covered, Muleshoe, 225 miles from Perryton, was in our district.)

There are still some old-timers in Perryton who remember more how Mike quarterbacked Max Baumgardner's East to victory over Buddy Fornes' West than they remember anything he did in baseball.

I might as well tell you about that Greenbelt Bowl game, because it will give you an idea of the way I was and am. Mike and I had been going steady since he was in eighth grade and I was in seventh. By the time Mike was a senior we had been steadies for five years.

Actually, being selected quarterback for the East was just the latest honor for Mike. He was also all-state defensive back and captain of the basketball team. He played golf as well and would have been a four-letter man if we'd had baseball. Not many big leaguers make it without ever having played in high school. I've heard many reasons for Perryton High not having baseball—windy conditions and dust storms, lack of area schools to compete with, inadequate facility. Finally in the spring of 1988 the school board voted to start a baseball program at the high school level.

In places like Perryton football was and is king. The Greenbelt Bowl was and is the annual coronation. When Mike was selected to represent our school and I learned a queen of the Greenbelt Bowl was to be selected from the girlfriends of the players, the coming game became less dramatic and more traumatic. We girls were to be in a parade (and this was before I even had my parade wave down) and interviewed by the judges. There was the inevitable beauty contest—one of those scary ones where you have to walk up on stage and be stared at by people you know are sitting out there saying, "Does she really think she's *pretty*," while you're walking across the footlights saying to yourself, "No, I don't. Give me a break. I never wanted any of this."

That took a lot of fun out of the Greenbelt. I couldn't care less about such things, but then again I wasn't about to suggest to Mike that he ask someone else to represent him. I figured that eventually I could be myself, sitting with Mike's folks and mine, enjoying the game. No way! We "beauty" contestants were expected to wear our long formals, long gloves, and high heels and actually sit on chairs on the sidelines. From Perryton to Williamsport, I have never been able to take a ball game sitting down. By the time Mike's team ran off its first series I was jumping up and down, screaming at the top of my lungs, my shoes plunked down under my chair.

Did any of the other girls join me? Of course not. They

This was my senior picture,
from our high school yearbook.

sat there demurely, clapping nonchalantly. But even the queen and her court lost their cool when Mike, with our team behind in the last fifteen seconds, threw a touchdown pass for the victory.

Nearly eight years later, sitting in Arlington Stadium among the other Ranger wives during Mike's rookie season, I set up a one-girl cheering section to root on the Rangers who, for the first time in their brief history, were in the race most of the season. I no longer remember what the message board flashed except that it was something or other that Mike's teammate Toby Harrah had just accomplished. I let out a yell, fully expecting Pam Harrah to follow suit. Instead she showed no emotion. After questioning her silence, I heard words I have never forgotten: "We're not all rah-rah cheerleaders like you."

For a moment, I was back in high school, cheering for the Perryton Rangers; back at the Greenbelt, wishing I could be myself instead of primping for the judges; back under the lights in places like Great Bend and Liberal and Geneva and Gastonia. I knew Pam Harrah was right then, and I know it more fully now.

I also know I can never change.

I met Mike at the firecracker stand the summer before seventh grade. He was working at the stand for his church. I was with my brother Al, who had just obtained his driver's license. In Texas in those days you could get your license at fourteen, and I would soon be getting mine. The only thing on Al's mind was how soon he could be dragging Main, and the only thing on mine was this darn cute guy who was waiting on me.

Al was getting flustered at my pickiness among the sparklers and cherry bombs. I didn't mind when he took off. Now I could check out the noisemakers and this great-looking guy. What we said to each other, if anything, has long since disappeared from memory, but something etched itself there. It may have been mutual.

That fall, sitting with the other junior high kids at the high school's first football game, I saw this guy I knew to be a buddy of Mike's approaching. He came right over to me. Mike wanted me to sit with him. The name barely clicked; I asked to be shown where this Mike Hargrove was sitting. The mental reminder clicked into place. I joined the eighth-grade group of which Mike was the center.

We didn't say a word. When the game was over, I thanked him for letting little me sit with big him—no more than any seventh grader's gratitude. He said "see you around." We may have walked three steps in opposite directions when, for the first time that evening, I was aware of the Hargrove voice directed upward to the Rupprecht cloud.

"Sharon," said the voice, kind of raspy even then, "do you want to go steady?"

I said what any girl would say to the kind of offer that, though heard at ground level, surely originated in heaven. Mike handed me a ring and off I went bending my ring finger just a tad so the oversize ring wouldn't fall off.

Although neither of the girlfriends at whose grandmother's I was sleeping that night had ever heard of Mike Hargrove, it was the principle that mattered. Not only did I have a steady who was an older guy, but he was a hunk.

Going steady was tough when you were a grade behind. We saw each other mostly going to and from the cafeteria. Smiles and hi's were about it.

One day Mike stopped me in the cafeteria. "Sharon," he said, "I need that ring back."

"Why? Don't you want to go steady any more?"

"No, it's not that. It's my cousin's ring, and now *he* wants to go steady."

In place of the ring, Mike gave me a silver pendant with M-I-K-E on the front. Mike has given me many "fuzzy boxes" holding lovely rings, but I still love that pendant.

Puppy love was all it was at the time. All our courtship amounted to was meeting Friday nights at the show. We didn't have a real date until he was a freshman. It was to the junior high prom. I could go only because I was an usher.

My daddy set some ground rules. I could go only if it was a double date. I had to be home thirty minutes after the prom let out, and if Mike honked the horn when he picked me up it was all off. There was no horn honking, thank God, and when I answered the doorbell, Mike handed me a corsage.

After the prom, we had a flat tire. Honest. By the time he got it fixed, we had only ten minutes to get home. We cruised to the baseball field (of all places), which was kind of a lover's lane. We parked but before we could even kiss we were interrupted by bright lights from what we assumed was a patrol car. Mike panicked and zoomed off—straight into a ditch that had been filled up by blow dirt from a farmer's land. It like to have buried the car, and my time was up.

Mike and his cousin Scott left me and Marsha—Scott's date—while they walked to town for help. Imagine my surprise when they returned with Mrs. Key, my second-grade teacher, who had brought her pickup and a rope. It was so embarrassing. She couldn't budge us. She drove us all to a farmer's house where she knew there was a tractor. I phoned both our parents, just hoping the two moms would answer, but it was my dad's and Mike's dad's voices I heard.

My daddy eased my mind a little when, after I doctored up the truth a tad, he said, "Sharon, I'm glad you were considerate enough to call, but what were you doing on the baseball field in the middle of the night?" I let it all come out. "I'm glad you told me that," he said, "because that's where I used to take your mother."

But it didn't help things at all when Mike couldn't start his car. The battery was dead. While he and Scott were seeking help, Marsha and I had played the radio.

Next day I went to my piano lesson as usual, and Mike called up my mom to apologize. Everything went smooth from that point. It's not always so good to be brought up in the same town as your beau's folks. But there it is. I've been in love with Mike Hargrove since seventh grade.

Recently I read one of those front-page surveys in *USA Today* that make me uncomfortable. Their sports pages are the best, but those front-page surveys are something else: always brief and always sensational. This one was about early dating leading to early sex. It caught my eye, as we have three girls.

According to the survey, 91 percent of girls who begin

dating at twelve have sex before graduation (maybe as a graduation present to themselves?); from there the percentages go neatly down: 56 percent of those who begin dating at thirteen; 53 percent of the fourteeners; 40 percent at fifteen; only 20 percent at sixteen (but lots of girls graduate at sixteen, so maybe they figure they might as well wait until they get their diplomas).

I don't mean to sound sarcastic (o.k., yes I do), but this article points the finger squarely at me, because I was only twelve when Mike asked me to go steady. My guess is that *USA Today*'s survey sample of twelve-year-old daters, if national, would be awfully small. For all I know, there are more adolescent girls in small Texas towns dating than in the large cities.

This I know. Dating—if that's the word—as Mike and I practiced it had several factors in the way of its becoming rampant sex. First, there was sports. Mike was always either playing or practicing. Even though we didn't have baseball, Mike was active in football and basketball, and he played a lot of golf on the side—if he had any "side" left. I kept almost as busy, doing a little of everything: cheerleader, drum majorette, flutist, pianist, school paper editor. And I had neat girlfriends all through school. There was never any time for wild sex or any other kind.

More important, in a small town there are few secrets. If, during our seven-year sort-of courtship, we had been having the kind of relationship that would bear out *USA*'s findings, we would have had all our friends to account to. Plus something even more important. Respect for—often fear of—our dads and moms runs high in this state, and it probably runs highest in places like Perryton.

You have to remember: this may have been the rebellious sixties in many places, but in Perryton only "thugs" drank beer and marijuana sounded like Tijuana, a notorious place that our fathers, who had been in the service, whispered about to our moms.

19

There's a story about my dad that I like to tell because it's so like him, and it will also tell you something, not about casual sex, but maybe about getting engaged and how casual *that* can be when a couple have been steadies since junior high.

To please dad, who wanted me to be sure that Mike was the one, I enrolled at McMurry College in Abilene while Mike was a sophomore at Northwestern State College at Alva, Oklahoma. They had their Easter break before we did and Mike drove over to Abilene. He stayed with a friend from Perryton in the men's dorm and I with my roommate in the women's. Honest. We went to a matinee—it was all we could afford—and just happened into a jewelry store. We saw some rings we liked before going to the show. The rings stayed on our minds, so we went back afterward to price them. We ended up making a down payment, obtaining the rings, and there we were: engaged without really thinking about it.

Where we come from you don't get engaged without telling your folks. We found a pay phone in the mall. I told Mike *he* had better tell mom and dad. Of course, as on our first date, it had to be dad who answered.

If you know Mike, it will be no surprise that he talked about everything in the world except what he had called for. He kept hemming and hawing. By the time he actually said, "G. K., Sharon and I just got engaged and we have set our wedding date on your anniversary," Dad told me later that he was so relieved that Mike wasn't calling to say I was pregnant that he didn't even care that we had gotten engaged without their permission.

Mike had to leave to go back to Northwestern that afternoon. There I was all of a sudden with an engagement ring, which, of course, I showed to everyone even though few of them knew who I was engaged to.

In case anybody should want to fit us in that *USA* survey, let me say that neither Mike nor I saw anything wrong with dating other people the whole year I was still in high school and Mike was a freshman at NWSC. From my side, these weren't heavy dates; mostly they were with friends of my brothers. Any time a guy would ask me out I would say I'd love to.

My folks really liked Mike from the start. Dad must not have counted my high-school-senior dates as amounting to anything because he insisted that I enroll at McMurry for at least that one year, just so I could be sure Mike was the one.

Now nobody since has talked much about anything that happened my two semesters at McMurry or, for that matter, Mike's three semesters at Northwestern, but there's something you should know. My brother Al was already at McMurry, and my other brother Benny was at Northwestern. Mike and I had eyes and ears—spies, if that's what you want to call them—at the respective schools.

Somehow I survived that year serving my dad's sentence. You couldn't get out of the dorm on weeknights without signing out to the library. I was real glad when, the next year, I could transfer up to where Mike was.

We were married during Christmas break of my sophomore year. I was nineteen; Mike was twenty. The date— December 27, 1970—coincided with my folks' twenty-fourth anniversary. When we jointly lighted a center candle from two outside ones, which we then extinguished, we were symbolizing our union.

We spent our honeymoon in Colorado Springs—just a couple of green kids from rural Texas. One day we got on the elevator at the Broadmoor to go down to lunch. We saw a bellhop carrying a dozen long-stemmed red roses. We laughed, knowing how all the rich people we were around acted and thinking the roses were probably just for someone saying have a nice day. When we came back from lunch, there were the roses, in our room, with a card: To two bright and shining stars . . . Love, Dad. Then we remembered. Dudley—Mike's dad—had made a toast after our wedding rehearsal: "To two bright and shining stars, from four proud parents."

That happened the second day. On the first evening, a waiter "corked" a bottle of champagne. He poured a sip in Mike's glass. We missed the point. Mike emptied the glass and asked for a refill.

We learned a lot of other things on our honeymoon, among which was that resolutions about never having a fight don't last long. Like about a day. I had left my hairbrush at home so we stopped at one of those drive-in groceries. I then did something we never did in Perryton. Realizing we were no longer in Perryton and had made it to Dalhart, which, although larger than our town, was hardly a metropolis, I locked the doors of our car. Nothing wrong with that except that the keys were inside. Mike calmly asked for a coat hanger. He managed it all with a sense of humor I couldn't help but contrast to my dad's top-blowing under similar circumstances.

I should have shut up while I was ahead. Instead, I blew it: "Mike, why don't you put the hanger in the trunk in case we lock the keys in the car again?"

Mike's response was logical but cruel when you consider I was only trying to be helpful: "If *you* lock the keys in the car, how can *we* get in the trunk to get the hanger?"

When does the honeymoon end? I have often thought about this, so many of the couples we are now with being newlyweds. Here is the conclusion I have come to: the sooner the better. You hear of so many early divorces that you have to assume that the next step after the honeymoon is not a period of learning and adjustment, as it has to be, but the divorce court.

There have been three especially tough times in our marriage. The first came during the first spring—the first ball season—after we had come back to Alva from Colorado

Springs. It was the worst by far of the three, but it ended up setting certain private terms our marriage vows didn't cover.

When we got back, the athletic department put us up in a small house on the golf course about five miles into the country from campus. The expenses were minimal, but we kept bumping into each other.

Bumping into each other literally and figuratively. As far as making a house into a home, I'm good at it. Out there on the golf course at Northwestern State was just the beginning of something I would be doing for many years. By the time I had zip-stripped the walls, painted the furniture, and "antiqued" a little, I had our first place as a couple looking good enough for our folks when they drove over to visit us. Some of the places we've paid rent on in semipro and Class A can't hold a candle to it.

In fact, I had shipshaped that house so well that Mike and his buddies on the Northwestern Rangers used it as a place to unwind. Not only was Mike co-captain his last year but he was the only married player. Something I didn't know about when I was leading cheers in high school and when I was just Mike's girlfriend his two middle years in college was peer pressure. All those years, if Mike needed a buddy, I was it.

Now that we were married, and I figured I would be his wife and best buddy all in one, I had a rude awakening. Mike's *other* buddies were Steve Hilterbran, co-captain and catcher, and about twenty other guys. In the majors there are all the other married couples; they are separated by long distances. In the minors, you're all in a difficult setup together, but it's not like college. In college, the players play together, drink together, maybe carouse together. Life is a kind of extension of the game.

And our little house became an extension of the locker room. To the guys it was a great place for them to sit around watching Monday Night Football and talking about baseball or whatever else was on their minds — if anything. And I was the clubhouse manager who took care of all their needs ("Like another beer? Have some homemade cookies."). It didn't take me long to see an object lesson in all this: I was their object.

Not only did I know very little about ball Mike's last amateur year; I knew even less about marriage. All I knew was that I was miserable a lot of the time. If I hadn't been so busy taking twenty-one hours trying to cut down the time between Mike's upcoming graduation and my own, I might have had more patience. As it was, I became less and less tolerant of Mike's nights out with the boys. Some code of wifery that I had always followed now followed me. I rarely discussed the problem with Mike. After all, I didn't wish to be a nagging wife. I figured if I kept my mouth shut, he would soon get it all out of his system and there would be an end to it.

Things between Mike and me just dragged on. I didn't nag and he didn't change.

One Friday afternoon near the end of the baseball season Mike and I planned on going home to help my folks move. My dad was in the savings and loan business and had received a promotion to manager of a new branch office in Spearman, twenty-five miles from Perryton. At the last minute Mike announced that Coach Perkins had called a practice for Saturday morning. I had never heard of Saturday practice, but I went along with it. I decided to go on to Spearman with a friend and Mike could come later. We planned to meet at Panhandle State on Saturday. There was a game there.

The meeting came off, but the rules had changed. Mike and his buddies had had a few beers en route. He was a little too cool when he joined me in the stands wearing his handsome letter jacket: God's gift to women.

He knew I wasn't taking this Mike in stride. He kept his distance until the game was over. Our plan had been for him to accompany me back to Spearman. With a nonchalance Mike has never exhibited on any playing field, he announced, "If you don't care, I think I'll just go back to Alva with the guys." "Well, I *don't* care," I spit out the words with more vehemence than I had ever shown in our marriage. I left the field and drove to Spearman.

"Where's Mike?" Mom asked.

I made a lame excuse but it was swallowed up by my tears. When I tried to tell Mom my sob story, she interrupted, "Don't talk to me about Mike. He's my son-in-law."

She stopped me every time I'd try to let it out. "Shary, I love Mike. So do you. Please find a friend you can talk to about your problems. You'll get over being mad and I might not."

Even though I knew Mom was right, I had to have someone to spill it out to. Finally, Mom got to the heart of things in that way she has:

Mom: Whatever Mike is doing that is bothering you, have you told him about it?

Me: Mom, I don't want to be a nagging wife.

Mom: You know, Sharon, some of these things you're upset about now will have a way of still going on twenty years from now . . .

Me: But I keep thinking Mike will see that I'm unhappy and stop all this.

Mom: Like I said and I want you to remember this: Mike's your husband, but he's our son, too. I'm just not about to get into this. I'll tell you again. Something's bugging you now is likely to still be bugging you twenty years down the road, especially if you don't let Mike know what it is.

And, you know, Mom was right. I had to let Mike know what was bugging me. First, though, he needed a little of his own medicine. I took my old sweet time getting back to Alva even though I hadn't prepared him for my getting back late.

When I arrived past 11 o'clock (with no phone call to let

him know I was going to be late), I found the house in perfect order. He had even fixed supper; it was still on low on the stove. I neither kissed him nor congratulated him on beating Panhandle State. I said I had already eaten and I was going to bed. At that moment Mike broke down in apologies: how sorry he was for the way he had treated me all weekend, how much he loved me. I never let him finish.

"Mike, don't *tell* me you love me until you can *show* me you love me. You didn't treat me this way before we got married and you won't treat me this way now. I married you to spend time with you and be happy. Well, I'm not very happy right now. I won't spend my life like this."

Mike never called my bluff.

Three years later, after Mike's first long road trip in the major leagues, he said he was ready to quit baseball right there at the start if it was going to make me so unhappy.

I didn't call his bluff either.

It wasn't a matter of bluffing. We both realized the honeymoon was over and we'd better get busy building a marriage.

Perspectives

Memory is a misleading thing. You look back and wonder in the Now how you endured the Then. It wasn't all that tough if you took a year— a day, a game, an inning—at a time.

There's an old saying in ball that covers a lot of territory. Veterans in this game insist that everything evens up. I've always thought that was something a manager has to tell himself to get some sleep at night. When his team is losing one barnburner after another, he has to tell himself that things will turn around. When his team is on a roll, he knows that an injury to a key player, a fly ball lost in the sun or the lights, a bad bounce in the infield—any of a hundred unforeseen things—can start the toboggan slide.

Our life in baseball is the same as the game itself.

If you didn't know Mike and me and saw in the record that for three seasons we had been coaching and managing in the low minors, you might think, baseballwise, that we had reached the pits. But that's the only kind of wise you would be. Another kind of wisdom that you only learn about when you've been bobbing up and down in baseball for twenty years is that nothing worthwhile comes easily and almost nothing comes overnight.

There are twenty-six big league teams, each with 24 players. That makes 624 names on the active rosters. I am not knowledgeable enough to know if it's true, as some old-timers say, that the quality of play is watered down by the sheer numbers of required players. What I do know, from the case of our own Tommy Hinzo, is that a player can be in Class A one day and in the majors the next. But few make it without paying their dues down here. Those who do usually live to regret it.

We are paying our dues. When Mike made the decision to stay in baseball after he failed to catch on with the Oakland Athletics as a free agent in the spring of 1986, he knew the terms of the new deal. He would have to start at the bottom as a coach just as he had had to start at the bottom as a player fifteen years earlier.

The minor leagues are where you learn, but what you learned as a player cannot be anything like the same as what you learn as a manager.

We have coached and managed at Batavia, Kinston, and Williamsport. To tell the truth, we're looking to something as dramatic to happen for us in 1989 as happened for us in 1974. You may already have read about it in the sports pages.

We truly think we are on a journey back to the Big Show. The journey is a full circle where we have come halfway—Geneva and Gastonia to the Texas Rangers and Cleveland Indians— on the field. Now we are navigating the other half—Batavia and Kinston to—who knows after Williamsport?

I want to describe the two halves in terms of each other. The next two chapters will be two-way mirrors that reflect backwards and forwards our beginnings in the roles of player and wife as well as manager-coach and wife. Each half will be clearer when held up against the other.

Even as we look on it, the full circle is closing . . .

Full Circling I

Batavia, New York (Summer, 1986),
Geneva, New York (Summer, 1972)

I T ' S a funny game. If anybody had told us back in 1972, when my husband and I broke in with the Geneva Rangers of the New York–Penn League, that fourteen years later—twelve of them in the major leagues—we would be back in the New York–Penn, I'd have said they were crazy. But in the summer of 1986, here I was, rah-rahing in the stands, this time for Mike's new team, the Batavia Trojans, just like I was doing then.

Of course, it's a different ball game. Mike isn't playing any more, and then I didn't have four kiddos hopping around. But the league's just about the same. The New York–Penn was listed in the *Sporting News* as Class A then, and it's listed that way today. Now the kids playing in Batavia know they're actually in a low Class A, as distinguished from, say, the Cleveland Indians' other Class A team, the Waterloo, Iowa, club of the Midwest League, which is a high Class A.

Mike called the New York–Penn a rookie league in 1972, and in 1986 it still was. These were all college kids—and even a couple out of high school—who were signed in the annual June draft.

You can't know the inner workings of professional baseball unless you understand the draft. Jim Piersall, who has
had his own problems in ball, used to refer to some of us
wives as "dumb broads," and for all I know there are some
of us out there who still think a squeeze play has something to do with hugging. But three facts of life in modern-
day ball that I have learned all about are the draft, multiyear contracts, and free agency.

Mike was drafted at the start, signed multiyear contracts
in the middle, and failed as a free agent at the end. Let's
try to nail down what the draft is, and hold the other two
for when they came up in Mike's career.

If you remember how Selective Service for the military
used to work, you'll have the right idea. Some scout gives
the kid a checkup just like your military medic looked over
the draftee. These days the scout's stethoscope is a stop-
watch that clocks speed or, for pitchers, a radar gun that
measures what everybody in ball now calls "velocity." You
would be surprised at how important speed is in an everyday player. The scouts figure it's God-given and can't be im-
proved by instruction. I once asked Mike's dad, who had
exceptional speed, what the difference is between speed and
something else you hear a lot about in the minors — quickness. Without hesitation, Dudley said, "About two steps."

Mike will be the first to tell you he has below-average
speed. That's probably why he was drafted in the twenty-
fifth round of the June, 1972, player draft. At the time we
were thrilled.

Everything starts with being drafted and landing that first
contract. The ones most of the college kids were signing
in the early 1970s were light years away from the big bonus
contracts you read about for the Bo Jacksons and guys like
that. Most kids who are assigned to Class A—in Mike's
day and now—sign for peanuts—about $300 or so every two
weeks.

Many of the kids Mike coached at Batavia won't ever

see a second contract. The good ones will be picked for the Cleveland Indians' Instructional League just as Mike was by the Texas Rangers. In the years between Geneva and Batavia I had clean forgotten the tension among the guys over whether they would be playing ball in October and November. As the season winds down in August, you can cut the tension with a knife.

In 1972 Mike was being watched. Now he is doing the watching.

Mike was thirty-seven in October, 1986, but I swear when I looked at him trotting out to coach at third base those nights in Batavia he looked the same as when he took the field at Great Bend, Kansas, in semipro. In Batavia he was coaching for Tom Chandler, mostly working with the hitters. Tom, who coached at A&M nearly thirty years and scouted and covered every diamond nook and cranny in Texas, was in his first year as a manager.

We liked it that way, working with another Texan who like us was doing something completely new that summer.

On those balmy Upstate New York evenings I tried to get the children ready early. We headed out to Dwyer Stadium about 6 o'clock for fielding drill and batting practice. There was old dad hitting fungoes to those rookies on the same diamonds where he was shagging 'em in 1972.

When he was playing for Geneva, Mike's name appeared in the lineup card at the fourth spot (the cleanup position), but in the Texas Rangers' press book he was listed, as I mentioned, as their pick in the twenty-fifth round and, what I didn't mention, the 572d player drafted overall.

At the time—June, 1972—neither of us knew enough to judge how little faith the Rangers were showing. As a coach, Mike plays on that today. When these kids in Rookie League get down on themselves, Mike just tosses his own unimpressive stats from Geneva at them, including a one-for-thirty-three start (he made a hit his first at-bat and then didn't hit anything the next thirty-two). He batted only .267 that year.

But memory often gets sugarcoated. Early in the 1986 season, when we pulled into McDonough Park, Geneva, for our first game against the Geneva Cubs, the public-address announcer remembered Mike: "Coaching at third base for the Batavia Trojans is Mike Hargrove, formerly of the Cleveland Indians, San Diego Padres, and Texas Rangers, who is returning to the same diamond where he started as the first baseman for the then Geneva Rangers during the 1972 season. Let's give a real Geneva welcome back to Mike Hargrove!"

Goose bumps broke out on me and, although he won't admit to such things, on Mike, too. To tell the truth, though, the Geneva P.A. announcer's words were far from accurate. Nobody starred on or off the field at Geneva in 1972.

You would have to have been a Pete Rose not to have seriously considered quitting ball after Geneva. In fact, Pete did start his career there, and he hit only ten points better than Mike. I'd like to ask him some time if he ever talked like Mike ("If I can't do it at this level," etc., etc.). What we were thinking in summer, 1986, was what we could say to Michelle and Kerry Richardson (our third baseman/designated hitter), who couldn't register for the fall semester at Lubbock Christian because they didn't know whether he'd get a call for Instructional League.

Looking back, I still can't figure out what kept us going that first year we had gotten our foot in the door.

Mike's announcement to all our folks that he planned to play semipro in Kansas the summer after our marriage was almost universally unpopular. Only his father really wanted Mike to go for it. Dudley had been a promising third baseman whose chances for the pros soured twice—once with the New York Giants when he had to go home to help with the harvest and once with the Brooklyn Dodgers when he got sick. Dudley never completely got over those two bad breaks.

The main opposition from Mike's side came from his Granddad Herman, whom we all called Papaw. Papaw allowed as how Mike was now a married man who ought to forget baseball and get a job with a future. (This was the same Papaw who subscribed to the Gastonia *Gazette* Mike's second season, when he was earning $600 a month on his way to becoming the Topps Chewing Gum Western Carolina League Player of the Year.)

We played semipro in the flatlands of southeastern Kansas two springs and early summers: 1971 at Great Bend and 1972 at Liberal. If you were a couple of hopefuls just out of Northwestern State College — if you were Mike Hargrove or Steve Hilterbran — you lived for the day some scout would see you play and recommend that you be drafted by the major league team he represented.

You've got to remember that this was 1972, more than two years before Andy Messersmith and Catfish Hunter took their owners to court and free agency changed baseball. It was also well before the colleges, even old NWSC, came to be regarded as a testing ground — another minor league, really — for young talent.

In 1972 there was just some bird-doggin' scout out there beating the bushes.

One Saturday afternoon Mike's senior year, between games of a doubleheader with Southwestern State, a man I had never seen before approached me in the stands. Mike had told me there would be big league scouts in force, filling the seats behind the plate. They were there to see Ray Burris, Southwestern's star pitcher (still in the majors until released in 1987 at the age of thirty-seven). But at least one scout — the stranger who approached me — liked the looks of somebody besides Burris. He identified himself as Lee Anthony of the Texas Rangers. The team — would you believe? — didn't really hit home because my knowledge of baseball was nonexistent in those days. Mr. Anthony gave me his card, which he requested I give to Mike. He then handed me a form, parts of which he requested that I fill out right there in the stands.

The items I filled out for Mr. Anthony on what I later learned was Mike's first scouting report certainly didn't help him. I hardly knew one base from the other; the game mystified me. All Lee Anthony wanted were a few stats under physical profile—those and Mike's position. I kind of panicked. For some reason I had it in my mind that six-foot was five-foot-ten. Knowing that Mike was a tad under six-foot, I wrote in his height as five-foot-nine. I know now that his weight—210—would have been just right for a man five-foot-eleven-plus but a bit excessive for someone five-foot-nine. Although Mike played first base in college, I checked the box that said "infielder/outfielder," thus crediting him with more versatility than left-handed players can have.

We heard nothing from Lee Anthony until after Mike reported to Liberal in June for his second semipro season. Everybody in baseball knows that some scouts will promise anything to get a signature. We were soon to learn that Lee wasn't that kind. He phoned Mike one day and promised he would be back later in the week. Mike didn't even ask what team he was scouting for. For reasons I'll never know, Mets stuck in my mind. Maybe it was unwishful thinking. New York was the last place we wanted to go.

Several weeks went by. Mike and his pal, catcher and co-captain Steve Hilterbran (Steve had also been contacted by Lee Anthony), were going crazy. About three weeks later, the phone rang. It was Lee. Mike was at work in a meatpacking plant. Lee gave me the news. The Texas Rangers had drafted Mike.

When I have good news to tell someone, I'm a world-class sprinter. The security guard wouldn't let me through the gate. I told him Mike had been drafted. I'm sure he thought Mike was heading straight for Vietnam.

Mike and Steve were on break. They spotted me just as

I spotted them. I began running and shouting, "Mike, you've been drafted by the Texas Rangers!" Nothing since Mike was named all-state in football was even close to the thrill on a June afternoon in 1972 at Liberal, Kansas.

When we came down off cloud nine, we realized, sadly, that Steve Hilterbran, whose dedication to making the majors went far beyond Mike's, had not received a call. Mike signed for a whopping $2,000 and was told to report to a place deep in Yankee territory called Geneva. We had a week to report.

It was mind-boggling. We would do it right. With the $2,000 bonus and $100 borrowed from Mike's dad, we traded in our old car and made a down payment on a Pontiac LeMans.

Now that we are parents four times over I can understand what our folks must have thought when we pulled out of Perryton. It must have hit my parents hardest. At least Mike's father had been a fine athlete with professional aspirations. Although my two brothers, Benny and Al, were gifted athletes, they had played sports no farther away than Northwestern State and McMurry.

This was unprecedented, seeing us off to New York for a fraction of what Mike had earned that winter pumping oil. But there we were heading straight northeasterly for the great beyond, where surely there loomed a baseball career, whatever that was.

You don't know about the interstate when all you have ever driven is rural roads in Texas, Oklahoma, and Kansas. We may have known about there being a AAA office in Amarillo, but we hadn't joined. It would have been nice to have had one of their trip tickets to show us the best way to travel the nearly two thousand miles ahead of us. All we had was a national road map that showed that the first big square between here and there was St. Louis. That map didn't show how those big interstates we knew nothing about can get you around rather than through. Try to remember your first time driving through a city the size of St. Louis. You learned quickly or you stopped. We stopped.

There was a Holiday Inn that looked just right for a couple heading for a career in baseball's Big Show. Besides, we had never stayed a night in anything like a big-city motel. We had been married barely a year. Most couples like us would have thought being alone in a Holiday Inn was real romantic. But *my* husband was about to start a career in baseball. He bought a newspaper and turned to the sports section. The Cardinals were playing at home that night.

Mike's excitement infected me, too. Our first big league game. We dined at a barbecue place near Busch Stadium then purchased seats that made Bob Uecker's look like boxes. (Seven years later—spring, 1979,—playing for the San Diego Padres, Mike took the field at Busch Stadium. He remembered the seats we occupied at our first game. He spotted the same barbecue place and dined there for old time's sake. One year after Geneva—1973—at the Rangers' Plant City, Florida, minor league camp, we would drive a few miles north to Lakeland to see our second big league game, an exhibition involving the Detroit Tigers. He saw two of his early heroes, Al Kaline and Frank Howard, play. Mike leaned over to me. "If I had to play fourteen years in the minors just to play in one exhibition game with guys like Kaline and Howard, it would be worth it." A year later he would be playing in the majors.)

Leaving St. Louis early next day, we took a longer look at our newer U.S. road map, which I picked up at the Holiday Inn. One of the few places east of the Mississippi River that I knew about was Niagara Falls. Without my knowing it then, I was putting together two ideas, one recent, the other longstanding. The recent one was that we would be somewhere to the other side of the honeymooners' paradise, and the older one was that I'd like before I died to see Niagara Falls with my husband.

Driving in Texas and heading, say, for Dallas–Fort Worth, you would have to figure on another couple of days if you wanted to make a side trip, say, to the Alamo. I didn't notice it at first, of course, but later that first summer in Upstate New York you couldn't help but notice how a driver, used to the distances in Texas, could travel the New York State Thruway, Buffalo to New York City, in a matter of hours.

From Geneva to Niagara Falls was like a Sunday picnic. We took in the Falls then just as we did again in summer, 1986 at Batavia, when we played at St. Catharine's, which is just over the border. Now we've seen Niagara from both the U.S. and the Canadian sides.

Coming into Geneva, you see a big sign: Geneva, N.Y., Lake Trout Capital of the World. That sign might as well have read: New York: THE Capital of the World. Like many Texans, I was in awe of being somewhere — anywhere — in New York. In those days I made no distinction between city and state. There was no way, in one season of ball in Class A, that I could learn to take Geneva — or any place in the Empire State — in stride.

I used to take the big sky over Perryton for granted. I don't anymore — not after Geneva. Everything in those New York–Penn cities is scaled down, it seems, and very old. The Texas Rangers reimbursed us for our gasoline, but nobody helps you find an apartment. Even when we settled for two rooms under an attic, we waited for the phone to ring presenting us accommodations especially set up for the players and their families.

Jane DiAngelo was our first landlady — the best. Jane, recently divorced, was bringing up her two children alone. Jane hated cooking and allowed me the privileges of her kitchen.

She was our first "civilian" friend that first year in ball. Back in the New York–Penn League, Mike and I stopped first at Jane's house. Later, when the P.A. announcer recognized Mike, she was with us in the stands. Between innings I walked up to a regular I remembered from the old days. Harlan Olsen didn't recognize me at first. When I identified myself he exclaimed, "I should have known. This is the only game I'll see all season. I had heard you were back in the league."

But it was like I said: Mike never got untracked at Geneva, and I learned to hear my husband booed. He hit only .267 in seventy games and felt like he didn't play well in the field. Nothing in semipro in the Kansas boonies had prepared us for the Geneva fans and how they roasted the home team when somebody made an error or tossed up a home run pitch or struck out with the bases loaded.

The kindest remark I remember was one offered when Mike let a batted ball scoot between his legs to lose a game: "Why don't you get a lunch pail and go to work!" Some of the unkinder ones I can't bring myself to mention. At least Mike was spared the special abuse reserved for pitchers: "Poke him with a fork and see if he's done!" "C'mon ragarm, you can pitch slower than that!"

I was having my own problems. Shopping for food was an adventure. In Perryton, I could always run up a big bill and say to the clerk, if I was short, "Just charge it to G. K." In Geneva, the first time, I bought $70 worth of groceries, tried to pay by check, and was refused because I had neglected to obtain a check-cashing card.

Then there was Hurricane Agnes, which hit Geneva broadside just after we arrived. Luckily, the city is high and drains into Seneca Lake on the outskirts. The Rangers had a series in Auburn, which is just west of Syracuse, when the P.A. announced an "extreme weather alert" and ordered the game suspended so everyone could go to their homes to await further directions. The dam was about to break. Within a couple of hours fifteen thousand people were evacuated. The dam held, however, although the heavy rains left hundreds of families temporarily homeless.

In Perryton, Wolf Creek is about all you have to worry about. Even after many years and traveling the length of New York State from Buffalo to New York and Jamestown to Albany, I still think of the state as hemmed in by water and about to be washed into the Atlantic Ocean or Lake Erie, at least.

I was just too dumb generally and put-upon domestically —yes, and self-centered, too—to see that Mike was having a tougher time than I. He kept saying he was ready to pack it in, go back to the oil wells in Perryton, or maybe ask Harold Wilson for a job at Central National Bank in Alva until he could get a job coaching in a high school.

You will recall how our folks—especially Papaw—kept reminding Mike that playing ball in the boonies was no way for a man to support his bride and the family we were sure to be raising. I would be lying in my teeth if I said the same thought didn't go through my head all season at Geneva.

There were lots of good times, too. We have never been anywhere in summer as lovely as the Finger Lakes. I especially remember the picnics with Charl and Jim Pascarella. Jim played infield for the Rangers. We would go mornings and early afternoons. We especially liked Watkins Glen and going for a swim. Living in the Texas Panhandle, Mike and I had lived through the sixties without ever laying eyes on a hippie. They had them at Watkins Glen, bathing in the altogether, and I remembered thinking it wasn't true that hippies didn't wash themselves. We saw them—plenty of soap, too.

In Batavia, in summer, 1986, there was no time for anything like picnics before games. When Mike got on the players for doing things on game days (what isn't a game day?), I'd tell him, "Lighten up! Remember Geneva and the good times we had."

A lot of wives detest having to sit around listening to the guys talking baseball, but we would sit around the table in Jane DiAngelo's—some of the players, a couple of wives, and us—having a midnight snack after the games (snack? Why, Jane and I would do full-course dinners!).

I had come a long way from waitin' tables at the Hargrove Hotel back there on the golf course at Northwestern State. It's different in the minor leagues. We're all in this together. I'd never consider talking baseball an imposition.

It was in Geneva that we discovered potato chips in a can—Pringles (perfect for picnics). But most of all I learned to love the rolling hills of Upstate New York. In Perryton you can stand on a beer can at night and see the lights of Chicago.

Speaking of standing on things, Geneva had the fattest telephone book I had ever seen, although we had to go to San Diego and Cleveland to find phone books thick enough to use for booster chairs.

Neither of us had ever been so far away from our comfort zone. The precious few long-distance calls we could afford were the only connection to our families. Remember these were pre-Sprint and MCI days.

One day Mom called to say Grandma Rupprecht had just undergone emergency bypass surgery. Mom promised to call back with a condition report. When she did, it was to tell me there were complications and Grandma was back in surgery. Somehow she survived.

How I survived my first season was just as unbelievable. If we were to stay in ball, I would have as much adjusting to do as Mike.

Despite his .267 batting average and the feeling he didn't play well at first base, Mike was invited to the Rangers' minor-league camp, Plant City, Florida.

We had our foot in the door.

In Batavia, fourteen years later, watching twenty-five kids reach for the gold ring that only four or five would grab— that is, an invitation to the Indians' Instructional League, Sarasota, to which Mike had also been invited—I kept remembering a certain good omen we had from the start.

I can't forget about Mike and his old Cleveland Indians uniform.

We had pulled into the Treadway Inn, just off the Thru-way, where we would be until our house was ready. Our only requirement in such transient accommodations after all these years is that there be a swimming pool for the kids. It was a Sunday in mid-June; the 1986 New York–Penn season was to start the next day. We met Tom Chandler, who drove us out to the Batavia Trojans' clubhouse. Locker rooms in Class A must all look alike to Mike, but this time Mike let out a cry, rare for him. He recognized the Batavia uni-forms as ones that had been worn by the Cleveland Indians the previous season. Somebody had removed the Indian in-signia from the shirts and hats—and, of course, all the names.

Mike kept checking out those Indian uniforms of 1985 that would be the Trojan suits of 1986. Finally he found what he was looking for: one of the shirts had "Hargrove" written inside the collar. "My God," he said to me that night. "One of these kids is going to be playing in my shirt and pants!"

I looked at him, knowing we were thinking the same thing. Back in 1972, when we reported to Geneva, we wives and girlfriends removed the Texas Rangers' players' names so rookies like Mike could wear them.

Mike always took the field in the uniform of a pro. About now you're probably thinking that coaching rookie hitters in a low Class-A league isn't that big a deal for a guy who played twelve years in the Big Show. Mike didn't look at it like that, and neither did I. Fact is, I get a good feeling every time I see "coach" after Mike's name. It's what I've always wanted. Mike was a good coach that season, and I knew he'd be a great manager. You could tell. There was this boy, Glenn Fairchild, who played shortstop. He wasn't hitting a lick and he was piling up the errors. He was sure

Tom Chandler was going to sit him down any day. Mike took Glenn aside and reviewed *his* start at Geneva. You remember it: a single his first at-bat and then zero for the next thirty-two, and still he played every game.

It helps to hear firsthand how somebody who has been there weathered a slump and still stayed in the lineup.

The seasons in the minor leagues are shorter. Two and a half months in Class A, just a little longer last season at Williamsport. If something should happen and there's no job next season for Mike, I would still be telling anyone who would listen that the game has been good to us. I wouldn't have given up these years for any other life. I won't forget any of them.

Instructional League is the closest thing to spring training baseball offers. I even took my name off the substitute teacher list for a week and visited Mike in Sarasota. That Gulf Coast city had always been one of our favorites. It was down there that Mike got the sensational news. He was being promoted to manager in high Class A. The Cleveland Indians were starting a franchise at Waldorf, Maryland, which is about as close to Washington, D.C., where we had never been, as St. Catharine's is to Niagara Falls. It would be great for us and the kids to see our nation's capital.

Later, though, we learned that the Waldorf franchise didn't pan out. Mike would be going to Kinston, North Carolina, instead. Kinston, we were told, is a good baseball town. Mike would have some of the same players as he'd had at Batavia.

Only this time he would be the manager.

Scoring

All summer at Batavia I watched Kim with the big score book in her lap. She has always been good in art, and there is something artistically satisfying about scoring a baseball game. For a long time I could never get the hang of it. I'd much rather lead the cheers. It was second nature for me—rah-rahing around in the stands—even with Mike only coaching at third base or sitting in the dugout.

I would be yelling my head off without the least clue why. I hear they have yell leaders at A&M even at the baseball games. They must know more than I did. All during Mike's four years playing at Northwestern State College, those two springs in semipro in Kansas, and even at Geneva we were so strapped financially that the last thing I ever considered was that baseball could be fun.

You don't think of baseball as a rah-rah sport. We didn't even have it at Perryton High. The appeal of football for a cheerleader type like me is simple. The game is simple. Eleven guys on one side trying to move the ball across the goal line of the eleven other guys. You cheer if your side is moving the ball, or you cheer when your side is holding back the ball.

Mike, whose first and maybe most abiding love is football, told me from seventh grade on that there's more to football. I could see that.

I'm a "made" fan of baseball, not a born one. But loving ball didn't come all at once. If you'll pardon me for stealing from that Frank Sinatra song, I did it my way.

Baseball became plain old "ball" for me when two things happened. I learned to score, and I found I could reconstruct a game in my mind from my score book. All during the dog days at Great Bend and Liberal, Mike would try to get me interested despite empty ball yards in the boonies of Kansas and nothing I could see to cheer about.

If you do it right, he would say, you will know afterward where the balls were hit, who caught them, and how the runs were scored.

First, you sketch in a little diamond in the square after the batter's name. Batter A makes it to first base. If it's a base hit, you insert a short line in the tiny space at that angle of the diamond. Two dashes, inserted at the appropriate spaces, means a two-base hit (double); three, a three-base hit (triple); four, a home run. The more dashes a batter has in the spaces after his name, the more he has contributed to getting himself or his teammates around the little diamond.

Under Mike's good-natured coaching, I came to think of the players by the numbers—one to nine—tradition has assigned to them. I had no trouble understanding the title of a book by the late Danny Thompson, one of Mike's teammates on the Rangers. Danny played shortstop—that's number six—so he called his book E6. That's right out of my score book—"error, shortstop."

I don't know of any other game you can score in a way that is both fully descriptive of the play and fun.

Mike played first base. Nothing happens in baseball until somebody reaches first base. It's like you make a deposit at first, but the dividends are paid at home plate.

It was fun when Mike showed me plays where baseball is most like football. The defense against the bunt when all four infielders and the catcher are moving. The way Mike is like a linebacker intercepting a pass, except that his job is to intercept—to cut off—his own teammate's throw from the outfield to keep baserunners from taking advantage—moving up.

You always hear that baseball is a game of inches. I guess you could say that of every sport where there are boundary lines. I think of ball differently. What you learn, when somebody just takes the time to clue you in to what to look for, is that it's like a smart-looking gal who has all the good equipment nature gave her except she uses the wrong eyeshade and has a run in her stocking. Somebody is sure to downgrade her on her flaws. Baseball people know how perfect a game potentially is so long as its symmetry is kept. The scouts see the grace and the flaws, and they report on who has the face and figure without the runs in the stockings.

Early in the 1981 season, Mike's third with the Indians, he phoned from the stadium to urge me not to try to make it to the game. A misty rain had been falling all afternoon and he thought the game with Toronto might be called off. I didn't mind not going; I was five and a half months pregnant with Andy. I turned on the radio in the seventh inning. Our pitcher, Len Barker, with whom Mike had also played in Texas, not only had a no-hit game going but nobody had even reached base.

I couldn't stand it. By that time I knew how rare such games are and how few fans ever get to see one. I gave it to Mike good when he got home. All he could think of was the wonder of having played in such a game.

"Most awesome thing I ever saw in my life, the only perfect thing in team sports. Twenty-seven batters, twenty-seven outs!"

What fun it would have been to score Len Barker's perfect game. At least there's a framed scorecard for that game in our trophy room. It's signed by everyone who played that night.

Full Circling II

Kinston, North Carolina (Summer, 1987),
Gastonia, North Carolina (Summer, 1973)

EVERY day with the Kinston Indians in what Mike calls
the "high" Class A was like Dionne Warwicke singing "Déjà
Vu." And, like an unforgettable song, everything kept coming back.

Watching those kids play under the lights of Grainger
Stadium, I was back at Gastonia, and it was 1973 all over
again. There was Milt Harper, our slugging first baseman,
tossing the ball to the other infielders at the start of the
visitors' at-bats. Milt's left-handed, and his moves at the
plate and in the field reminded me of Mike, his second year.

Hearing Mike and Steve Comer (hasn't Steve got the perfect name for a coach—aren't we looking for just that, a
comer or two?) . . . hearing those two buddies from the
Texas Rangers days gab about how this guy had the tools
but lacked the temperament to make the Big Show or how
that one needed to shorten up his bat stroke or add another
pitch, I caught myself speculating about how the Texas
Ranger brass must have discussed Mike's prospects after
his award-winning 1973 season at Gastonia.

Mostly, though, I listened to the wives. In Batavia there
were only two couples on our team. There were a half dozen

47

at Kinston. I was looking into that two-way mirror again. I saw myself in them. A gap of fourteen years closed. Did I talk the way they did?

Early in the season, Cleveland moved Rod Nichols, our best pitcher, up a notch to Williamsport, Pennsylvania. That's double A; the big team could be next. Rod's wife, Sharon, had to stay behind a few days to pick up the leftovers. Somebody has to do it when a player gets moved during the season. Somebody has to explain why you can't stay as long as you said you would.

But there, sitting with us wives and girlfriends behind the plate and the big protective net, was Sharon Nichols. This was already a couple of days after Rod had departed for double A. Sharon Nichols saying goodbye to her friends. A really neat thing to do.

Wait a minute. She stayed the whole nine innings, complaining all the while about how God-awful her day had been. Closing out the bank account, shutting off the power, the phone, the cable—doing all the nuisance things we wives in ball know about. These girls have enough to worry about that their guys *won't* get moved up. I just wish Sharon would have cooled it a bit. But who can blame her? She and Rod had just paid $67 for a phone jack and now were departing ten days after installation. They had just had the cable hooked up. Having the cable is not a luxury for guys who live the night hours ballplayers do. They had just opened a bank account, paid for the minimum number of checks you can order—eight hundred. When Rod was called up, they had written twenty-four. Sharon had just found a job the day before through a temporary-job agency, which is the only outfit through which our wives can apply, because everybody knows they won't even be in Kinston through the summer.

Mindless jobs at minimum pay. That's about it. Girls like Michelle Richardson and Chris Ghelfi (Tony Ghelfi actually pitched in three games with the Phillies in 1983; he was drafted in 1982 and was coming back to ball from two arm operations) are college women. They and the others are not Barbie dolls. Michelle couldn't wait until she could finish her teaching degree at Lubbock Christian so she could teach, hold a real job. She had just learned that Kerry would be going to Instructional League, which was good for him, not so good for her. Six more weeks of temporary jobs through November. Chris Ghelfi was one of the rare ones. She had put everything on hold to see Tony through his attempted comeback.

We had it better at Gastonia. I don't remember anybody being moved up. What we didn't know didn't hurt us. Compared to the twenty-one-year-old greenhorn from the Panhandle, with one sixty-game schedule in Rookie League under her belt, these wives were really into baseball—and its politics. All they talked about was being "moved up," their husbands' chances of making Instructional League, avoiding another Kinston experience.

The Carolina League schedule was harder, too. At one point our team played fifty-four straight nights. I don't remember Mike being away overnight much when we were in the Western Carolina League. I saw most of the away games; I doubt if our wives went on a single road trip. I only made one trip—that to Prince William, Virginia—so we could take the kids to Washington.

If the manager's wife can't make the trips, how can working wives?

I know some of them had to be afraid, alone in trailers, outside town. I really admire how they endured these separations of four to seven days all season. I couldn't have cut that.

Some of the girls had never heard of a tornado watch, a commonplace in Kinston. The Richardsons lived in a trailer. Have you ever lived alone in one of them during heavy rains when there's a tornado alert? Michelle's lights went out one night while Kerry was on the road. She had a flashlight, but fifteen minutes was all she could take. In her shoes, in a trailer with four kids, I'd have collapsed in five. She phoned. Would I mind if she came over? She spent the night.

There's this picture I still have, a kind of set scene for ballplayers' wives. I woke Michelle at 4:30 the morning after the tornado alert so she and Kim, our oldest, could meet the team bus. Michelle hadn't seen Kerry in three days and Kim hadn't seen her father in three months (she had stayed in Perryton to finish sixth grade and had just joined us in Kinston). Maybe an hour later, I woke up, the rising sun shining into the shadeless window of my room, as Mike and Kim entered the apartment. I told myself once again that I must get some shades for that window.

And, of course, there was a game that night.

None of the wives could believe that I was happy in Kinston, especially after, as they say, smelling the roses. They all knew how little Mike made as manager. They also knew that the major league minimum in 1987 was $62,500, and could only guess what Mike must have been drawing after a dozen years in the majors.

I saw a lot of jealousy and envy—especially among the pitchers' wives. Who can blame them? Mike was a position player and a regular from the git-go. I think it is harder on you if your husband is a pitcher; harder because there are nine other pitchers. It's like your husband is in a special class—both senses of the word. The competition is fearful. If your man is getting belted around as a starting pitcher or gives up the winning hit in the last of the ninth as a relief man . . . and that other guy keeps winning or rates some such tribute as "stopper" . . .

Baseball's Great American Game image is tarnished the most by those fans who think instant money, not to mention fame, makes instant happiness for the players and their families. Fans wouldn't be so resentful if they understood.

One night, during that one road trip I took with the

team into Maryland and Virginia with the kids, we sat in the stands of the Prince William Yankees, a farm club of the New York Yankees. I noticed that Juan Bonilla was on the Prince William roster. Now Juan must have been at least thirty, having played three seasons on the San Diego Padres, although not so far back as 1979, when Mike was briefly there. He had been a major league regular as recently as 1983. Mike told me Juan had dropped out of baseball in 1984, tried for a comeback in 1985, led Columbus (the Yankees' triple A team) in hitting, only to be released by the big team that year. He had hooked on again with New York but had been sent down as far as you could go.

In the bleachers anywhere in the boonies it's not hard, with a trained eye, to spot a woman whose husband has played in the Big Show. There's usually an area, close to home plate or behind the home team's dugout, where there's a protective screen. Even in the low minors these sections are reserved for the wives. After all these years, in any professional yard in America, I could walk to these sections blindfolded.

Most wives, especially in places like the Carolina League, don't pay much attention to the game. They tune in only when their man is pitching or hitting. What all we baseball wives do best is chatter. I may be the biggest chatterbox of all. However, some of us, like scouts, have trained eyes; we don't miss a trick. This night in the stands at Prince William I surveyed our wives' section: gals in blue jeans, some with their babies, all looking alike.

Mike, who really likes him, says Mickey Mantle had a Cadillac strut when he rounded the bases on a home run. There's a Lincoln Continental look about some baseball wives that sets them apart, even in a capacity house.

The woman whom I focused on that night wore diamond rings and held a designer handbag. She also looked more "dressed"; her skirt was longer, more stylish; the kids a little older. Surely she was Juan Bonilla's wife.

I'm not usually shy, but I didn't approach the woman with the prosperous look until the next night, after Mike had arranged for me to have a seat in the reserved section. She was pleased to meet me and have someone who knew how hard it was, in places like the Carolina League, after you've been in the majors. Yes, Juan and she were surprised, after his big year at Columbus the previous year, to be in Class A. It was just temporary, the New York Yankees had assured him. (The Yankees did recall Bonilla in late July to fill in for the injured Willie Randolph at second base. However, upon Randolph's return, Bonilla was sent again to Columbus.) She didn't know what she would do if Juan didn't make it back up. They had exhausted their savings.

Later, when I got home and looked him up in the Baseball Register, I learned that Juan Bonilla, like Mike, had played in both leagues. He had five seasons — full or part — in the majors.

Jean Bonilla said she wasn't the only ex–big leaguer's wife at Prince William. She pointed down several rows to a girl, whose name I won't mention, who she said was taking it even harder. All I know is that this gal was sitting — desperately? — alone, literally dripping in jewelry, with sculpted nails, the inevitable designer bag, overdressed in, of all things, a black jumpsuit and high heels.

What I saw that night, right out of one of those women's magazine style sections blowing up next season's most chic fashions, was what most people see when they think of us baseball wives. The TV shots are supposed to look casual, but even our kids are carefully selected for their antiseptic look. There's no way TV can convey the truer billing of most of us as women who love baseball and all it has given us and our kids without changing our real priorities as wives, mothers, homemakers.

We were really happy in Kinston. Occasionally, something really exciting happened. Take the story of Steve and

Kathy Comer and the sensational break we are all still talking about.

The sports pages listed it under "Transactions, baseball, Cleveland Indians: Fired Jack Aker, pitching coach; appointed Steve Comer, Kinston, Carolina League, pitching coach."

The squib probably went unnoticed even by the participants Aker and Comer, who by then were out of, or into, their new roles. Few fans, even baseball nuts, paid any attention. How many of them could have named the old pitching coach of the Cleveland Indians, let alone the new one? Or any pitching coach anywhere?

The date would have been July 1 or 2, or even later, depending on how quickly the Indians' media publicity people got out the word. By then, at a place geographically remote from Cleveland—a city of less than twenty-five thousand named Kinston, a city whose team had no major league affiliation a year earlier—certain tremors of that transaction shook up a few people wearing game uniforms —and their women—for about forty-eight hours.

For a precious few of us down in the boonies of baseball, it was news of the first importance. When anyone moved up a notch—to Williamsport, Pennsylvania, in the double-A Eastern League—it was worth a headline. It had happened to Tommy Hinzo, our all-star second baseman; to Doyle Wilson, our catcher; to Rob Swain, our shortstop; and, as I mentioned before, to Rod Nichols. When the Indians jumped Tom Hinzo through the roof by bringing him up at midseason to the big team, Mike noticed that suddenly his players were reading the major league box scores. What happened to Hinzo might sometime, someplace, happen to them.

Every player lives in the hope—often the illusion—that he is upwardly mobile. Hope is all he can hold up against the $350 paycheck every two weeks, the long bus rides in the middle of the night, the sure knowledge that he is low man on the totem pole.

When there are fifty-four games without a day off, as happened the first two months, former big leaguers like Mike and Steve also live in anticipation that one day the phone will ring, and it will be Mr. Danny O'Brien, vice-president of baseball operations, on the line from Cleveland.

Then it happened.

Steve Comer's appointment as Mike's coach was one of the biggest pluses for coming to manage Kinston. Mike and Steve had been teammates on the 1984 Indians. Steve and Kathy lived near us in Cleveland, just as they did at the Heritage Court Apartments, Kinston. The four of us were real close. That closeness would be tested when, during the first two weeks, Steve had a brouhaha with one of his pitchers so serious that he told Mike he thought he couldn't help the team. Mike talked him out of that, convincing him that he would not be a pitching coach in Class A for long. He could not have guessed it would be less than three months. I could not guess that my friendship would be put to the test during the forty-eight hours between a Tuesday evening and a Thursday lunchtime.

My account will be short on the transactional side that unexpectedly returned Steve to the majors but long on the domestic/logistical. What follows are matters that every veteran baseball wife knows about with scary intimacy but that their husbands usually take for granted in the bliss of professional ignorance.

Mike and Steve had departed for Grainger Stadium at 2:00 P.M., as usual, although the game with the Peninsula White Sox wasn't to start until 7:00. Steve was his usual thoughtful self in driving back from pregame drills to bring Kathy and me our June paychecks, which we, as usual, desperately needed. We had a visitor from Cleveland that week — Natalie Prusak, who had been our babysitter in Strongsville during the Indian years. I had not missed a home game all season but had decided to take a night off to work on this book. About five minutes before Natalie would have walked out the door with the kids to drive to the game, the phone rang. Kim answered. It was Dad, and he was in his office. Nothing alarming in that—although during our playing days, Mike hesitated to use the clubhouse phone. Now he was an executive, with office and private line. He frequently called before the game.

"Sharon," he said, "you've got to wake up Kathy. She must have her phone off the hook. Steve needs to talk to her. Something *really* important . . ."

I believe I suspected from the start that Steve had been called up by the Indians. I also know that baseball players have a special sense of secrecy about news—the good and, especially, the bad. The players want to hear it from the manager, not see it on TV or read it in the paper. The wives want to hear it from their husbands, not from another player's wife.

"Let Steve tell her."

The matter of confidentiality is vital concerning transactions. We would quickly be told that Steve was learning of his promotion before Jack Aker, his predecessor, had been notified he had been fired.

There are leaks everywhere these days. If you watched the Iran-Contra hearings you know all about leaks in high places. You just try to avoid having them traced to you. Cleveland is hundreds of miles from Kinston, but the telephone is a swift bearer of gossip.

Kathy's situation took on urgency when we learned that Cleveland wanted him up there the next day. If Kathy had no children, was in the best of health, had lived out of suitcases rather than, as wives like us always do, set up housekeeping for the season in a large apartment about one hundred yards from ours, and didn't have all those closing-up details the young wife of the transferred player had complained about at the start of this chapter—if Kathy had none of these, she could have flown up there with Steve next morning. As it was, she had two-year-old Maggie, whose birthday was the next day and for whom lavish arrangements had been made for a birthday party; she was five months pregnant and already beginning to have problems; and had a gigantic amount of packing to do if she were to meet Steve in Cleveland where, one somehow felt, no housing arrangements had been made by the Indians.

I tried to act casual with Natalie and the kids, remembering Mike had said no one—absolutely no one—was to know before Kathy heard it from Steve. I left the kids in Natalie's care, and when out of their sight broke into a 100-yard dash to the Comer apartment. Kathy was on the phone (does anyone talk longer on the phone than baseball wives, especially when calling loved ones from their new locations?).

Somehow I got it across that it was urgent she break off with her mother-in-law and call Steve. I watched Kathy's face with the built-in empathy of one who instinctively knew how she would receive the news. Women go through change of life once; baseball wives go through it every time their men are moved during the season. I looked to see the way her face would change: anxiety to joy. But it wasn't like that at all. She didn't believe him. "Bucky [that was what Kathy called Steve]," she said, "please don't lie to me. It's not funny. Are you tellin' the truth?" It was slow to sink in. Later Steve told Mike, "You see what a trusting relationship the Comers have."

As soon as she hung up, we grabbed and hugged each other, not exactly crying, just sobbing, for joy.

"He can't even say goodbye to his pitchers. They haven't told Aker yet. Steve's already booked on a 10:30 flight to Cleveland in the morning."

All this was the most exciting thing that had happened

This shot of Andy illustrates "living out of
a suitcase," a phrase baseball families know
all too well.

to us in Kinston since our arrival in April. You won't believe what was going through my mind as we clung to
each other. I'm sure Kathy, who had had about as many
moves as we'd had, was thinking it, too. Steve had to hold
back, sit through maybe a three-hour game, then come
home and try to get some sleep. As it was, we also knew
that she would not have a minute she could call her own
—it looked to be beyond reach—if she was ever to sit behind the wheel of their van, knowing that the bills and
claims, all the loose ends, wouldn't be following her to
Cleveland.

Nothing happened in Kinston—off the field, that is—as
exciting as the Comers' unexpected jump from Class A to
the major leagues. Mike and I like to think of Kinston as
bridging the gap between retirement as an active player and

return to baseball as a manager. Kinston, in short, was a gap closer.

In 1973, not so far from Kinston, Gastonia closed the gap between civilian life and baseball life.

Between our first and second seasons in organized ball, Mike worked for a lumber company in Alva while I completed my student teaching for a degree in elementary education. That spring of 1973, Jim and Charl Pascarella, who had been our best friends at Geneva, drove cross-country from East Haven, Connecticut, spent a few days with us in Perryton, and the four of us headed in separate cars for Plant City, Florida, the Texas Rangers' minor league camp.

The Rangers' farm director was a huge man who could intimidate you every time he opened his mouth. His name was Hal Keller, one of the few people in ball whom I was scared to death of. The Pascarellas and us—in fact, most of the kids at Plant City—were trying to get by on $500 a month. Somehow I persuaded Mike we couldn't live on that. He should go see Mr. Keller and ask for $800. We got $650. This was the first of many compromises, the heart of even six-figure negotiations. At the time, $650 seemed like a lot of money.

We finally found a duplex at $85 a month. We were on one side, Jim and Janet Sundberg on the other. Jim, as the baseball world would soon know, was a catcher with, as they say in baseball, "all the tools." Jim and Janet have been our close friends all these years, but at Plant City what stood out about them was that he had been the Rangers' first-round draft pick the same year they had taken Mike in the twenty-fifth. Jim had received $10,000 to sign. The Sundbergs were driving a beautiful LTD.

About all I remember about Plant City is the roaches (our first experience) and a colorful guy Mike called Two-Tone Tony, who took care of the team's bats and had liver spots. Tony was the first guy in ball to predict that Mike Hargrove would make the Big Show in a hurry. Mike,

though, will tell you *his* biggest thrill that spring was seeing Arnold Palmer play.

Our manager at Gastonia was Rich Donnelly, whom
Mike considers the best manager, overall he had in ball.
Rich, who has been a coach with the Pittsburgh Pirates for
several years, was voted manager of the year for three of
his first four minor league years, an accomplishment I doubt
has been duplicated in minor league history. Rich's assis-
tant was Ed Nottle, who later coached with Oakland. A real
comedian, Ed. What was really serious at Gastonia were
the two big signs in the outfield. Any player who hit the
ball out at those spots would receive $100. For folks like
us who had about $20 left from our bimonthly check, those
signs promised sheer magic.

Our income stats, although somewhat better than the
$2,000 total we made at Geneva, were nothing to write
home about.

One day, waiting for the game to start, I saw a cleaner's
truck pull up to the clubhouse. All the other wives had regular day jobs; only a few showed up for the games. The Hargroves were head over heels in debt. When I spotted this
cleaner's truck a little light bulb went off in my head.

Immediately I went to the front office. I offered to do
the team laundry for half what they were paying the company. I would charge fifty cents for uniforms and five cents
for towels. They went for it.

Until we became established, I told Mike to be sure to
stomp on any towels he saw, clean or not. So desperate were
we that I may even have said I would gladly accept as tips
any change the players left in the pockets.

All that first full summer in ball Mike stowed the uniforms and towels in the car after each game, and I played
laundromat.

Mike hit .351 that second year (sixty-one points higher
than the next best), had a five-for-five, and was named Topps
(Chewing Gum) Western Carolinas League Player of the

Year. I've long since memorized his stats, which were impressive, including one that Mike never came near to equaling again. For a blue chipper both at quarterback and defensive halfback, Mike was never blessed with his father's speed. But that year of 1973, at Gastonia of the Western Carolinas League, Mike made double figures in stolen bases. He stole ten, double his best in twelve years in the majors.

Our first fully positive year in ball had sorrow, too. Grandpa Papaw died; Papaw, who had been Mike's toughest opposition to trying for a baseball career; Papaw, who subscribed to the Gastonia *Gazette* so he could follow the box scores of every game his grandson played.

Rich Donnelly tried his best, but the Rangers would allow only a single day for Mike to fly to Perryton for the funeral. Mike declined, not wishing to see his granddad off so hurriedly, even if we could have afforded the airfare.

You don't play ball without resentments against management. Sometimes they fester. Mike has never put his first behind him.

It Takes All Kinds

As far back as girlfriend spats in junior high, I remember Mom saying, "It takes all kinds, Sharon. Be yourself and let everyone you meet be themselves."

If I could remember having trouble getting along occasionally with gals who had been brought up in a small town like me, talked like me, dressed like me, had the same values, what lay ahead in baseball, where you are thrown in with women from all parts of the United States? If I was to enjoy life in baseball, I knew I had better accept the mix.

Where I grew up, people really mean it when they wish somebody, "Have a good day." A response like the one I heard the other day—"Sorry but I have made other plans"—would go clear over the heads of most of us Perrytoners. I was brought up in a place where awareness and concern are the way of life, and Southern Comfort is not a sickly sweet beverage.

When we landed in the Northeast the first time, I experienced culture shock of my own over how rude and abrupt Upstate New Yorkers seemed. I've learned that the opposite side of that coin is that you never have to guess where you stand. Unlike back home where people will call you sugar, honey, and sweetie to your face and then stab you in the back, my friends in Geneva, Strongsville, Batavia, and Williamsport will— as one of them put it—always let you know "where I'm coming from."

It was on the other coast—in San Diego—that I found people whose freestyle lives included not giving a rip what I was doing.

In Texas everybody I knew was on a first name basis. In Ohio, I felt hurt and old when the kids on the block started calling me "Mrs. Hargrove." I attributed the formality to my being Mrs. Mike Hargrove, the wife of a baseball celebrity. Then I discovered that my kids were also being rude without intending to be when they called the neighborhood moms by their given names.

I was "Mrs. Grover"—Grover is a nickname stuck on Mike by Bobby Jones, a buddy from the Ranger days—at the yard. In Kinston, I became "Miss Sharon," which I admit is one of my favorite calling cards.

I also had to adjust to the various ways people say things. When the kids wore jeans in Kinston, they were "youngins in dungarees." When they needed to catch a ride to school, someone was always only too glad to "carry" them. *Y'all* gave way to *you guys* or *youins*. When I said I was *fixin'* to go to the game, people looked puzzled wherever I was, although I've heard newcomers to Texas, after a few of our hot summers, say as if to the manor born that it's *fixin' to rain*. I never knew how to order a big sandwich: was it a sub, a hoagie, a grinder, a hero, or a bomber? Did I get a pop, a coke, or a soda at the game? What was the vendor trying to sell when he kept yelling, "Reds, get your reds!"

Basically, though, I have found people to be alike all over this country. No one I have ever met likes to empty the dishwasher or fill ice trays. No one is ever patient if I don't go immediately when the light changes to green. No one is ever satisfied just to get in line at the market unless they are sure they picked the quickest, shortest one. Very few stay in the line they picked first time.

I like people. I have never had a problem making friends. I consider myself gregarious and try to understand people who think that's a fault. When I am away at holiday time, I am the one who asks others in the same boat to come on over. One Thanksgiving I got carried away. I ended up with thirty-three invited guests. This was after Gastonia in 1973. I was concerned, until a guy who understands my sense of humor intervened: Rich Donnelly, Mike's manager and our best pal, phoned that morning to determine if his green parking pass could get him within five blocks of our place. Later, Mike walked into the kitchen carrying an Air Traffic Control sign.

Then I knew that with a few laughs most days will go as well as I expect them to.

Home on the Rangers

I THINK I have a pretty good memory, but I try not to play around much with hindsight. Hindsight is the game you play with yourself to change — in your mind, anyway — the final score that circumstances totaled up for you. It's all the business of if I knew then what I know now. Ballplayers hate when the writers keep bringing up old scores. Mike says you go nuts in this game second-guessing yourself when the first guess is what went into the books. You don't need any help from the writers.

Memory is kinder — for me, anyway. It's like refinishing old furniture. If you did a good job, only the shiny result shows. You forget how that old table looked.

I'm calling 1974 our vintage year, the best of its kind. But I'm going, like they say, with the flow — the furniture varnish, so to speak: my 1974 scrapbook, Mike's Rookie of the Year fame, our first "big" money, my self-image as the wife of a big leaguer, and Mike's as a sports celebrity, at least in Texas.

Adding a glossy refinish like that to the record can't blot out from my mind more important things: my first experience with the death of someone close to me, the loneliest days of my life, the growing fear that I would never make

it as the wife of a baseball star in the making, my first
pregnancy.

If I had 1974 to do over again, I would have done some
things different. But like I said, I don't play around much
with hindsight. Except in this book.

Despite some nice letters and plaques and a big write-
up in the *Sporting News*, that off-season—our last in the
minors—boils down to one afternoon in late winter. There
was a postal pickup note with our mail; one of those "you
weren't at home but can pick up a registered letter" teas-
ers. It was addressed to Mike. I just couldn't wait overnight.
I phoned Irvin Hergert, our postmaster. He met me at the
post office and opened up. Registered letters and Perryton
are not exactly close acquaintances. But when one comes
along, we Perrytoners are luckier than in the big city. We
can get around regulations.

This one looked important. It had "Texas Rangers American League Baseball Club" in the upper left-hand corner.

I had never seen a registered letter, let alone received
one. Mike was out playing basketball in the Y league and
couldn't be reached. I felt like it was my duty not only to
go get it but to open it.

It was an invitation from Billy Martin, manager of the
Texas Rangers, to attend their big league camp at Pompano
Beach, Florida, in February.

I got right on the phone. I guess I called everyone I knew.
They all heard about it before Mike did. I don't think he
got to break the news to anyone.

We were going to spring training with the big team.

I forgot to mention that, as soon as the Gastonia season
ended, Mike and I both got jobs. I accepted my first full-
time teaching job in the grade school while Mike tried to
sell crop insurance. For him, the air ticket to Pompano
Beach, supplied by the Rangers, marked his first time ever
in a commercial airplane. I never wanted anything up to

that time as desperately as to be with him. I still had memories of our cross-country drive in the Pontiac to Geneva and the drive with the Pascarellas to Plant City. Something in my strong Methodist upbringing—that and the watchful eye of my dad—obliged me to honor my teaching contract.

Gilbert Mize, the superintendent, did give me a week off, but except for what was actually more like a long weekend, I did not see Mike from February until early April. It was the most we had ever been apart in our three-year marriage: a sneak preview of what lay ahead.

Mike would phone me every night. Spring training with the Rangers was the first time that I experienced late-night telephone conversations. If you're a ballplayer's wife, don't let anybody tell you the phone is a poor substitute for in person. Mike and I said things to each other—intimate things that our enforced first separation oiled up for us—that, to this day, we don't say on the scene.

Of course, there were the rookie things—about what it felt like to hit against big league pitchers. Even technical stuff that I didn't understand had words that were like sparks to my loneliness.

Mike was really scorching the ball in Florida. He was enthusiastic without being carried away. Typical Mike. The scores from Florida would tell you one thing, Mike another. "It doesn't mean a thing," he would say every time. "Jim Spencer will be playing first base and Jim Fregosi will be D.H.ing [designated hitter]."

On those days he didn't get to play, I'd try to cheer him up. But from start to finish of the Ranger years Mike never questioned a management decision. Well, maybe the final season he did. If I gave in to hindsight, maybe I could see where Mike ought to have made a few waves.

He would always tell me to keep checking the Dallas papers for the news that he would be sent down. I swear Mike didn't believe they would even tell him.

Baseball people will tell you that those spring exhibition games don't mean anything. But when you're a rookie and hitting .522 going into the final week, everything is serious. That spring the Rangers were scheduled for a three-game series with the Houston Astros to decide braggin' rights in Texas. As things turned out, the Astros won all three games, 7–6, 7–5, and 5–4, but those scores didn't mean anything.

Mom and I decided to fly to Houston to see Mike play. This wasn't my first sight of the Astrodome. Jim and Charl Pascarella—and Mike and I—had stopped for the tour a year earlier on our way to Plant City. I remember we attended a Charley Pride concert, and I took a roll of pictures and got nothing but the bald head of the man sitting in front of us (wrong dome). (Later, at Pompano, someone pointed to an agile-looking young man in an unnumbered uniform during infield drill. "That's Charley Pride. He once tried out with the Milwaukee Braves. You always see him working out with the teams during spring training." Mike, who had never asked for an autograph before, gave in this time for his Aunt Kathy, who was a rabid fan of the singer. He gained more than Charley Pride's autograph. He learned from something Charley said about needing to be grateful that fans care enough to ask. I've never seen Mike refuse a request for an autograph.)

Mike's dad also flew in to see his son fulfilling his own ambitions. We got a big break. Jim Spencer had a strained arch, so Mike started the Saturday game. He had a great series. He hit doubles in all three games, went five-for-twelve, with five runs batted in.

Mom and I were thrilled with our complimentary seats. I've hardly known anyone who wasn't thrilled at the Eighth Wonder of the World, at least the first time. But Mike's dad said indoors is no place to play baseball. Later he and Mike would talk about the hollow sound the ball made, like you were in a big round bottle with the cap on, like you couldn't spit on the Astroturf without thinking you ought to mop it up. You could tell indoor baseball wasn't all that big a deal for Mike.

What was a big deal was that he was still on the thirty-five-man Ranger squad, which had to be cut to twenty-five by opening day, less than a week off.

Mike showed us David Fink's "Extra Innings" from the *Dallas Times Herald*, which, at the bottom, had Mike all packed off to the Rangers' triple A in Spokane: "Mike Hargrove, the big Native Texan first baseman who tore up the Carolina League last year, will jump all the way to triple-A Spokane this summer and a year from now may make a successful bid for the Rangers. . . . He has size, reasonable speed and looks good both at bat and in the field." That was in the paper Sunday, March 31, and we read it just before heading for the Dome and the final preseason game. Mike didn't play in the field, but he hit a double as designated hitter that tied the score in a late inning of a game we lost, 5–4, in the ninth.

We all flew home kind of hoping Mike might get a stopover in Perryton on his way to Spokane.

Next day, on the eve of the season opener, Mike phoned from Houston. It was the most excited I had ever heard him except maybe the morning he made all-state at defensive halfback. Now his news was even more thrilling. He was one of three rookies Billy Martin had decided to keep on the twenty-five-man roster. The others were Jim Sundberg and infielder Mike Cubbage.

That morning Mike had been unable to stand the suspense. He walked over to Billy Martin on the field and asked when the Rangers were going to send him down. Billy said the Rangers were keeping him but that if Mike objected he could reconsider. That was April 1, and both Mike, talking to Billy, and I, talking to Mike, at first suspected it was all an April Fool's joke. But Two-Tone Tony, the Plant City batman, had been right about Mike Hargrove.

68

Next day I went in to see Gilbert Mize and practically got on my knees to ask for a few days off again so I could be with Mike for opening day. He was wonderful about it. I only went back for a couple of days later before asking out of my contract altogether. I knew I would be no good with those kids, that Mike needed me backing him up. That's the way it would always be with us in baseball.

By mid-April Mike had found an apartment in Arlington. For the next twelve years neither he nor I—nor we and the kids who were to follow—would ever be separated except briefly when Mike's team was on the road.

It wasn't easy that first spring, and I wasn't even pregnant.

After the wonderful news that Mike had made the Rangers and after seeing the season's opener and watching a couple of games later when Mike, coming in as a replacement for Jim Fregosi at first base, got his first major league hit off Rollie Fingers (the umpires stopped the game and presented the ball to Mike—what a thrill!), I had to come down off cloud nine and face the Rangers' departure for an eight-game swing through California.

I had never in my life been alone before, let alone in a strange city. Arlington is no New York: while not a metropolis, it is a booming city located amidst some of Texas' busiest intrastate highways between Dallas and Fort Worth. In Geneva, I'd had Jim and Charl Pascarella; Rich and Peggy Donnelly were our best friends in ball then (at Gastonia) and now. In the minors, at the Rangers' minor league camp at Plant City and even at Pompano Beach, where I set up housekeeping for a precious week, there was a we're-all-in-this-together informality I have always loved.

The first week in the majors—the eight days Mike was on the road—was the longest of my married life. It got so bad I was afraid to leave the apartment. Once, daring to step outside for a stroll, I spotted a familiar face. It was Kathy Jenkins. I had known she lived in our complex somewhere and may have seen her at the games. Her husband was Ferguson Jenkins, a pitcher, one of the veteran players whom our new owner, Brad Corbett, had brought over from the National League — the Chicago Cubs — where, according to Mike, he had had some real big years.

What Mike really talked about was the amount of one of Fergie Jenkins' paychecks. It was for around $10,000 — and for just two weeks! Fergie had displayed the check to give rookies like Mike encouragement. His gestures had been intended to have a you-too-someday effect. Now here, doing her laundry, was Kathy, the wife of the richest Ranger. Without waiting for any preliminaries, so lonely was I, I blurted out something about could she and I maybe go to the show together. Kathy smiled but declined. "I'm sorry, we're already over our budget for the month. Maybe some other time."

I was devastated. I didn't buy that stuff about her being over their budget. Ferguson Jenkins' wife had refused to go to the show with me because I was a rookie's wife and she the wife of an established veteran.

Actually, as I have come to learn, Kathy's excuse was valid. What a lot of growing up I had to do. Mike, too, would make large salaries as he became an established veteran, and I would find that I had to budget as carefully when we were earning $450,000 as that first year when Mike signed a split contract for $16,000 ("split" in the sense that if he was sent down he would play for considerably less than $16,000, the major league minimum in 1974).

Whenever I page through the first of the scrapbooks I have kept over the years, it's a wonder I couldn't have fed off those columns that were devoted to Mike his rookie season. I wasn't at all sophisticated about what we in sports refer to, with good and bad memories, as the media. The *Dallas Morning News'* Randy Galloway took Mike to his heart from the start, his biggest booster throughout the five years with the Rangers. The headline on his very first column on Mike was "A Long Way from Perryton." It ran the length of the first sports page and closed with the prediction that Jim Spencer, who had missed the early games with an injury, "may have trouble getting his position back."

I won't say, at the time, I gave it the importance it deserved. Maybe I liked the spotlight of the headlines too much. A two-page handwritten letter, posted from LeRoy, Kansas, arrived in Arlington toward the end of June. It was from Lee Anthony, almost to the day two years after he had signed Mike to a Ranger contract. Lee was still beating the bushes of Oklahoma and Kansas, mentioning some names of guys Mike had played with in college and semipro but most of all congratulating the kid he had discovered on the year he was having, despite "such limited experience." Lee asked to be remembered to Steve Foucault, Mike's Ranger teammate, the team's top relief pitcher, but in Lee's view, having drafted him after seeing him hit and play third base in a junior college tournament at Grand Junction, Colorado, a potentially outstanding hitter whose true talents were being wasted. (When Mike retired, he sent Lee Anthony a wristwatch as a token of appreciation. It's easy to bask in the moment's spotlight and forget the ones who dredged up from deep in the bushes the professional-to-be.)

Mike had made it. At the end of April, the Rangers went into New York for their first series with the feared Yankees. In the three games, they never got Mike out. He had six hits, including his first big league home run, and three bases on balls. We won two of three, and Mike was the talk of the town. I wanted so much to be with him up there I could taste it. The schedule showed the Rangers had one more swing through the Eastern cities. I determined to make that trip.

I used to dream such fantasies all that first spring and early summer. If you were religious, as Mike and I are, it just didn't seem right that Mike should be in California and I all alone during the Easter season. After all, this was our first Easter with a common faith, as I had taken Instruction the previous fall and become a Catholic. I don't think I was foolish enough to think that God would grant me an airline ticket to Los Angeles. Mike phoned from Anaheim late after a game the Rangers had lost to the Angels in which he had not played. I determined to write him a letter—I still have it—undated (I hadn't yet learned to date everything; that came later, when I started keeping scrapbooks) and on sickly chartreuse-colored paper.

My choice of color was not random. I knew Mike would make the connection; he hated the green sofa—the one I kept staring at through those early road trips—as much as I. I mailed the letter to Oakland, the Rangers' next stop.

My dearest husband—

I love you so much and I really hated to say goodbye again. I loved being here with you. I'm so very proud of you honey. I don't know what I'd do without you. You're so good to me & treat me so special.

Please don't get discouraged about not playing. Who knows maybe you'll get to play today. You'll get in there & once you do you'll do just fine.

I'll be listening to all your games on the radio. Be a good boy—o.k.?

When you get home I'll be here waiting on you & the apartment will be like home then, won't it? I can hardly wait to get everything put up. I love the apartment, especially the green couch!

Take care, sugar. I know that I'm so anxious to see you & get to live with you again. My life has been so empty these past few months. Hope yours has been too. I'm not complete without you.

God bless you. Please try to go to Mass on Easter Sunday—o.k.?

Be careful & good luck on your trip. I'll be anxiously waiting for you.

Your loving wife,
Sharon

72

That first letter to my husband, the major-leaguer, was supposed to buck up his spirits. I really wrote it to buck up mine.

The surface of our life that first year was what the headlines, the stats, the awards, the Texas Rangers' runner-up position could bring to a sheen. They showed that Mike battled Rod Carew much of the season for the American League batting title; that he, playing in 131 games of the 162, did as much as anyone to make the Rangers contenders for the first time in their short history; that he was *Sporting News* Rookie of the Year.

What my life was really like could best be written in the mileage meter of our car; I was forever hauling somebody to or from the Dallas–Fort Worth airport. Or my life could be judged by the way my checkbook never balanced (I had never kept a checkbook before); or by the way my heart would race when I'd get home from shopping and wonder if I had missed a call from Mike. Or it could be judged by the appearance of my name in the visitor's book on seventh floor of M. D. Anderson in Houston, where my dad—the beloved G. K. to his kids and to all his friends—lay mortally ill of inoperable cancer throughout the late summer and fall.

Visitors were constant that first year, as often as not unannounced. It never occurred to us old-home-place Panhandle Texans, who rarely locked our front doors and never our cars, that we should get an unlisted telephone. I learned, often clumsily, to protect Mike from well-meaning but actually frivolous calls, from requests for tickets, from the occasional cranks who claimed his drawn-out ritual at the plate was actually slowing down the games (maybe they were right occasionally). I learned to put off the media after night games so Mike could sleep.

I learned to protect Mike, who was and is a setup for a favor even when it might hurt him. I could have used a guardian angel myself. But what angel is there to protect a twenty-three-year-old expectant mother from loneliness?

In Geneva and Gastonia, the seasons were short and so were the trips. In the majors the season is the longest in sports; 162 games in six months plus. There were ten road trips that season—each eight to eleven days. That comes to just about half of the 180-day baseball season, 90 to 100 days alone, in an apartment I detested when Mike was on the road. I wanted from the first to be a model baseball wife, but I felt more like a rookie in my league than Mike ever did in his. Where the model wife, so says Roger Kahn in *Joe & Marilyn* (1986), "lays aside individual ambitions and sublimates them to the service of her husband, the star," he is supposed to have as off-field standard equipment an ego that must be protected at home or on the road. Let me quote Mr. Kahn in full on the model baseball wife because if he's right I didn't qualify in 1974, when Mike broke in, and I don't now either, when he's managing:

> When a ballplayer travels, a model baseball wife busies herself with chores and bridge games with other baseball wives so that loneliness and depression do not attack her healthy smile. She recognizes that a traveling ball club is a world of young bucks and she is careful not to intrude. Young women, some lusty, some desperate, some both, materialize magically around baseball teams, anxious to surrender their chastity. . . . These ladies were called camp-followers in DiMaggio's playing years, groupies today. It is a rare ballplayer who can consistently resist these roadside models.
>
> The model baseball wife accepts her husband's casual philandering as part of the package she acquired when she married into the major leagues.

Not this "model" baseball wife.

One night, during either the first or second road trip, Mike phoned. Like I said, the only dividend of separations in ball is those precious half hours on the telephone, which, I have to admit, are among the best conversations Mike and I ever have. But on this particular night Mike owned up to having danced with one of those "slut puppies"—that's Kathy Comer's term for baseball's camp followers. Mike excused himself on the basis that she was an older gal, not really pretty, who he could see was lonely. He felt sorry for her. I had never heard anything like this from Mike. Sure, there had been beers with his teammates, but never any mention of dancing in bars with someone not his wife. Unlike in the first few months of marriage, I couldn't help letting it all out. My rage—or anguish—came out in a torrent. Didn't he know he was putting himself in a vulnerable position? How would he like it if I hit the bar circuit in Arlington?

"That's different," he said. "Girls who go to bars are just looking for guys."

"Yeah," I said. "Looking for guys just like you."

You're going to think I egged him into a chastity vow right there on the telephone. That's what many little old gals with strict Methodist upbringing like mine would have done. What I tried to do, after I'd let off steam, was to ease up, change the subject, and ring off on a good note. Something like my instincts that wifeliness is not prudishness took over. Mike may have had a bad day.

Still, I fussed over what he had said and I didn't sleep much that night.

To tell the truth, I was three kinds of jealous that first long season: of Mike for all those long trips to glamorous places ("You envy that?" he would always say. "You like standing around in airports and hotel lobbies? So much for all those glamorous places."); of Mike for never having to long for company (When the Rangers were home, there were more people around than anybody could wish for. When they were on the road, everything came to a dead stop. I have a favorite aunt who taught me to pin up notes on the

bathroom mirror: instructions to all those casual guests
Mike attracted that first year. Still, it was preferable to have
lots of company in the apartment rather than being stuck
there alone and afraid to wander outside.); of all the sophisticated wives—like Kathy Jenkins and, later, Blanche (Mrs.
Gaylord) Perry. I hated living in an apartment complex from
the git-go. Then there was our new owner, Mr. Brad Corbett, who was young and had a young wife, Gunnie. They
would soon be special friends. But that first year, I envied
them their big house and the country club they belonged
to. (Later, ironically, that club of Brad Corbett's would be
the scene of one of our most miserable times in ball, but
in the summer of 1974 a place like that seemed like the
answer to a lonely wife's longings.)

I am one of those people who need people. Once I got
up enough nerve to drive to Fort Worth, there were June
and Maurice Hargrove, a great-aunt and uncle of Mike's. I
visited them a lot. I was gaining confidence—and weight,
too. For this was when I learned that next season I would
not be alone during these dreaded road trips; I was expecting our first child.

Billy Martin prohibited wives from going on any of the
Rangers' chartered flights. He was even thumbs down on
having a wives' club. All those restrictions are pretty much
down the drain in the 1980s, except, that is, for wives on
the team bus; that's still a no-no.

I did, however (as I had promised myself), make one trip
that first summer. Janet Sundberg and I flew to New York
City. Our friends from the Geneva days, Jim and Charl Pascarella, invited Mike and me to visit them in East Haven,
which is near New York. The Ranger-Yankee series came
just prior to the annual All-Star Game, which is the tradi-
tional halfway point of the season. We would have some
flexibility because there is always a three-day break.

It was in East Haven that I found out what close-knit
Italian families are all about. "There are more Italians per

capita in our part of Connecticut than any comparably sized community outside of Italy," Charl told me. In our entire lives, before and since, Mike (who's from a huggin'-kissin' family) and I never saw so much of both. And the food! Nothing like it even to this day.

It was during my first trip to New York City that Brad and Gunnie Corbett invited us to dine with them at the Sherry Netherland. They even sent us back to our hotel near Central Park in a horse and carriage. Jim and Mike were totally embarrassed. They had the driver drop us off two blocks from the hotel so none of the other players would see us.

Thinking back to it, I don't doubt that I needed to get out of Texas altogether. It hits home to me how bittersweet that whole time was with the double-barreled knowledge that even as my dad was dying a baby was growing inside me.

Maybe it is always this way, life taking away with the one hand and replenishing with the other. I have always been grateful that God let Dad live long enough to see his only daughter's first child.

Was there ever a better time to be living in Texas than the 1970s? It wasn't like New York or Chicago or Los Angeles, where the limelight can burn a ballplayer out. That might happen to a football player in Texas, but baseball was so new here that neither the fans nor the media could kill a career. There's only one "America's Team" here, and no self-respecting Cowboy fan would think of heading for the exits in the fourth quarter like Astro patrons do in the seventh inning. Some of the best baseball fans at Arlington Stadium are old-timers who followed the old Houston Buffs or Fort Worth Cats in the Texas League. Some of the newer ones do more picnicking and socializing than caring about the game.

Spending the 1986 and 1987 seasons in the minors, I noticed that what's lacking in leagues like the New York–Penn and the Carolina is city-versus-city rivalry. We knew hardly anyone who would follow the home team on the road, even though the distances aren't great.

I think if the two Texas teams—or even one—ever got into the World Series, baseball would be born again here. Why, there would be a musical to compare with *The Best Little Whorehouse in Texas* or a night soap like "Dallas."

Baseball's not show-biz yet, like in L.A., or serious business, like with George Steinbrenner in New York. It was just right for us breaking in. I even started to come out of my shell to become again the outgoing person I've always been. I wasn't any longer going to be one of those wives who hankered after that last kiss whenever the team hit the road.

I couldn't stop altogether singing those sad songs. My dad, after all, was dying. I just wasn't taking myself so seriously.

What helped more than anything was the way Mike was taking *his* initiation in stride. I really began appreciating his quality of not-changing-ever, which I had taken for granted. Being around four females all these years may have made him a tad more sentimental, but there are much worse things. He could have been a jock to the core, real macho, even arrogant, overconfident. Mike couldn't be any of those things. To this day, he'll almost apologize for entering a room. Once I heard him, in that raspy voice of his, say "Turd!" when some guy was showboating it while running out his home run on TV.

There have been more sensational rookie years than Mike's but not too many times where an everyday player makes it from Class A in one jump. Ranger general manager Danny O'Brien told the media that Mike's rise was comparable to a high school football player graduating and signing immediately with the National Football League. Texas sportswriters understood that kind of comparison.

Mike and I have learned not to start wishful-thinking

this game to death. You start moaning the it-might-have-been-thus-and-so blues and you wind up just sadder, not wiser. We made it through our first season on Mike's $16,000 big league minimum. Brad Corbett did not renegotiate it, and nobody thought of the bonus considerations that are all the rage today. In the off-season, even before the *Sporting News* named Mike 1974 Rookie of the Year in the American League, Brad took him aside and said he should look up the highest salary ever paid to a second-year player and he would top it by $1,000. And he did too. And no agent was necessary.

I didn't hire a clipping service that first year. I know all that stuff about how the "ink" players in the big mass markets rate compared to the players in the smaller-media markets. Mike drew what can only be referred to as a "loving" press. There's a paragraph in the Rangers' media guide for 1975 that sounds corny yet catches the hometown-product-makes-good spirit that followed Mike all the vintage season: "It's Hollywood. It's Frank Merriwell. It's cow-jumping-over-the-moon stuff. It's unbelievable, but Mike Hargrove did it. And he did it where his home folks could see it—right here in Texas."

This is as good a time as any to say that Mike Hargrove put Perryton on the map, even though one of the Ranger play-by-play announcers kept putting an "i n-g" in there, making it "Perrington." Of course, between Mike and his hometown, the feeling was mutual. He was such a favorite son that Jerry Garrison and his radio station KEYE, Perryton, wanted to sponsor Ranger games and needed eighteen backers. Jerry made eighteen telephone calls and got eighteen sponsors.

Normally KEYE signed off at 10:30 P.M., but not when Mike Hargrove was playing.

Our KEYE isn't the biggest station going in West Texas by a long shot. It used to operate on 1,000 watts days and

This is Mike autographing a ball
during his great rookie-of-the-year
season in 1974.

drop to 250 nights, which meant if you happened to live more than twenty miles from Perryton you'd have to hope for perfect weather conditions—that means no heavy winds on our prairie—or tune in WBAP, Fort Worth, to hear how Mike was doing. Our folks estimated KEYE just wasn't able to bring in the night games more than two days a week.

The merchants in Perryton—those eighteen faithful Mike Hargrove boosters—paid the line, that is, the telephone, charges. It came to $60 for three hours. If the game ran longer than three hours, KEYE was in trouble. The merchants, etc., bought two "spots" per broadcast for a whopping $3.75. That came to a nightly take of $67.50. If the game ran over three hours, KEYE lost its $7.50 profit.

The first in line was Perryton's Kentucky Fried Chicken

franchise, which was then operated by Lanny Hargrove, Mike's uncle. At the end of an interview early in the season with Jerry Garrison, Mike was asked if he had anything to say to the folks back home. He did, urging them "to eat a lot of Uncle Lanny's fried chicken." That portion of the tape ended up as a commercial.

Near the close of the season, the Rangers arranged a Mike Hargrove Day. For two days, Saturday and Sunday, September 13–14, it was really Perryton Time at Arlington Stadium, because the Ochiltree Chamber of Commerce manager Leo Meyers chartered two buses, which carried eighty-two of our friends to see Mike perform against the only team ahead of the Rangers in the standings, the Oakland A's. A one hundred-seat section was reserved not only for present Perryton people but for others who had moved to the Dallas–Fort Worth area.

Billy Martin was "platooning" Mike — that is, he would hold him out of games where Mike, a left-handed batter, would have to face left-handed pitching. Mike did not start the game in his honor because the A's ace left-hander Vida Blue was pitching. Fortunately, the Rangers shelled Vida, and Mike came in early, thrilling his fans with a perfect sacrifice bunt to score a runner — a "squeeze play." The batter surprises the defense by shortening up on the bat — "bunting"— giving himself up while the runner is "squeezed" in to score from third base. He met his hometown fans in the morning, signed autographs, and had what up to then may have been his best days in ball.

For a soft-spoken country boy, Mike is also a battler. I don't think many rookies have had as many on-field fights. Baseball fights don't amount to much. Mike took on Jack Brohamer of Cleveland during a game at Arlington after Indian pitcher Milt Wilcox "dusted" Mike's teammate, Lenny Randle. Lenny challenged Milt, and the teams ran at each other. Mike took on Brohamer to protect a teammate. Or so Mike said at the time. Our most vivid memory is of a newspaper clipping someone sent us from *Montréal-Matin*, describing the fight in French. The story's headline quotes Billy Martin, who as you might expect was in the middle of it, describing the fight as "une bonne bataille pour nous" (a good battle for our team). The Rangers had been in a slump. Later in the season Mike almost came to blows with Sal Bando, the A's third baseman, who Mike thought deliberately stomped on his foot running out a hit. When the Rangers played in Cleveland, a fan spit in the direction of Jeff Burroughs, and Mike tried to join Jeff going after a bunch of unruly spectators. That time the Indians were about to help Jeff and Mike against the fans. Peace was quickly restored.

After the A's beat the Dodgers in the World Series, Mike took a job selling cars for a prominent dealer in Arlington. We received the word on November 25 that the *Sporting News* poll had voted him American League Rookie of the Year. A couple of days earlier UPI awarded him the same honor. Mike took the news with his usual modesty, telling Dallas *Times-Herald* writer James Walker that it was a good thing he was able to handle American League pitchers better than he was handling his off-season job. "If I had hit the way I sell cars I'd still be in A ball. Boy, this is tough. I'm hitting .000 . . . 0 for 28 . . . I've been here 28 days and haven't sold a car."

It was a dream year for Mike and a dream year for the Texas Rangers. There are five major individual awards after each season. Our team got four of them, the first and last time that has ever happened. Besides Mike's Rookie of the Year, Billy Martin was named Manager of the Year; Jeff Burroughs Most Valuable Player; and Ferguson Jenkins Comeback of the Year. Fergie finished second to Catfish Hunter for the Cy Young (best pitcher), or we would have made a clean sweep.

Through it all, Mike was viewed by teammates and fans alike as not having changed. I, of course, knew better. He raised his sideburns just a tad.

Here Miss Texas has just presented the Rookie of the Year Award
to Mike, as his mom and I look on.

Every Season Has a Reason

I can easily get carried away lining up the game
of baseball with the game of life. You can go too
far. I know a fan who takes baseball as a life-and-
death proposition. He admitted to me that he
couldn't imagine having a good day if his team
lost. Fortunately, his team is not the Cleveland
Indians. He would be having a barrelful of low
days. Now you can't have read up to here if you
don't know I'm as gung-ho for Mike's teams as
you could ask. But when the game is over, it's
over. If that sounds like something Yogi Berra
might have said, bear with me.

All I'm saying is that all these guys, from our
Tommy Hinzo, who made the Indians barely out

of his teens, to Phil Niekro, who was picked up pushing fifty from the Indians by Toronto in hopes he could help the Blue Jays win a pennant, are all grown men playing a kid's game.

You remember that when something really life-changing happens. You especially remember it when that life-changing thing happens at the very time, in terms of the smaller game, you are on a total high.

When Mr. Mize gave me a week off to be with Mike at the Texas Rangers' Pompano Beach training camp, I was flying higher than the jetliner out of Amarillo en route to Miami. Today I will do anything to avoid coming into the Miami airport in winter. I'll choose Fort Lauderdale or West Palm or almost any place to that madhouse. But in March, 1974, our first separation having stretched out to nearly three weeks, I was at the drawbridge of Camelot and there was Mike, a face-reddened knight errant, about to carry me across the moat. I would have other kisses and hugs over the years, bestowed at awkward hours in near-empty airports in Arlington, San Diego, and Cleveland, but none since was like this one: our first reunion after a long separation.

The whole Pompano week was like its beginning: romantic, heady stuff. I wrote earlier about how Mike's hitting was the talk of the camp, although Mike kept insisting he would be farmed out to Spokane. I sat in the wives' section at the games, looking at kids with books and tablets — youngsters I just assumed belonged to those wives — making up the work they were missing in their schools back home. It must have been then that I saw the self-contained Kathy Jenkins, wife of the great pitcher Fergie Jenkins (I had even heard of him), whom Brad Corbett had brought from the Chicago Cubs to spearhead the Rangers' upsurge. I determined to model myself after her.

Plant City and its cockroaches had never been like this. In fact, nothing in ball or out is anything like spring training in the major leagues.

When my week was up, I was down: lonely, disenchanted. Was this baseball, wherever we might go: a series of goodbyes at airports? What kind of life was I letting myself in for?

Something in my makeup won't abide depression for long. But what pitched me from the slow train of a general downer to the express of specific panic was the presence at the airport of my Aunt Rita rather than my mom, as planned. Rita tried to be casual. My dad was in St. Anthony's Hospital, in Amarillo, and Mom was with him.

That was the beginning. When I got to the hospital, I relieved Mom so she could get some sleep. I sat with my beloved daddy, showing him at his insistence the Texas Ranger media guide but fearful all the while of what I would learn.

I did not have long to wait. That same afternoon a nurse came in and asked Dad to sign a release for surgery next morning. He asked what they intended to do. It was then that I heard the word which to this day I cannot hear without dread: *tracheotomy.* Dad refused to sign. I could hold it all in no longer. I doubt if I had ever before combined disapproval and questioning of anything my father had ever done. When I now did both, he told me to mind my own business.

I phoned Mom. Al, the older of my two brothers, arrived first. We looked up and found Dad's physician, who explained matter-of-factly the purpose of the surgery. Dad's windpipe (trachea) was blocked. He was having trouble breathing—understandable, we were told, because the trachea is the principal passage for conveying air to and from the lungs.

When I asked the doctor what they expected to find, he spoke in a manner I thought at the time was too cold, too expressionless but which I have come to respect: "Your dad's a heavy smoker. With smokers, what we find is usually very bad."

And it was. The tracheotomy disclosed a spot on the lungs. Immediate surgery was called for—six to eight hours' worth. When the same seemingly emotionless doctor summoned us a little more than an hour later, my dad's blood visible on his green surgical smock, we prepared to hear the worst. The cancer was too widespread for surgery. Only Mom had the presence of mind to ask that cold fish not to tell Dad that the cancer was terminal, that he would live only three to six months.

Against our wishes, the doctor told Dad the gravity of his condition. Perhaps, in his way, that man knew G. K. better than we. Dad's determination to "beat this thing" was unquenchable. He tried, God knows. What he did beat was the calendar of his sentence. That extension allowed him these privileges, all precious: seeing his son Al happily married; attending many games in which his son-in-law made it that sensational rookie year; earning a major promotion himself and opening a branch office of the Savings & Loan, the company he worked for his whole life.

Most of all, God allowed him to become a grandfather.

The day I found out my dad had cancer I remember needing to be by myself. I went to the hospital chapel and prayed for strength. I began saying the Lord's Prayer, as I had done daily ever since I could remember. On that day I not only recited it, I *claimed* it for the first time. When I said "Thy will be done," my mind, my heart, my thoughts — my life — stopped. I made a commitment — one far beyond anything I had done in the physical church, beyond anything I had pledged to a minister or a priest. I vowed that if it were His will to take my dad, I would accept that.

As Dad lived through sheer determination six months, nine months, a year beyond medical expectations, I thought again of the words "Thy will be done." It cannot be in Your will, I prayed, to let him suffer any more.

The last time I saw Dad was just over a week before he died. I did not wish to go back to Arlington, but he insisted. Somehow Dad, whose son-in-law had only been in the majors a little over a season, understood about road trips. He insisted I be at the airport when Mike got in.

His last weeks were spent at M. D. Anderson in Houston — on the seventh floor. He hadn't been able to leave his bed for some days. We all knew the end was near. I knew how much Dad would wish one more time to see Kim, who was three months old. I tried to sneak her onto the elevator, but we got caught.

Mom found me in the lobby, crying. She tried to cheer me up with a plan the nurses had worked out. They were going to lift him out of his bed, prop him up by the window. I carried Kim outside, looked up, and there he was . . . waving.

Just before being driven to the airport to catch our Dallas flight, I said a final goodbye to the second most important man of my life. He handed me his watch, which kept falling off his wrist—how thin his arms were—and asked to me keep it for him. He then instructed me to take $100 from his billfold and buy Mom a pantsuit. Her birthday was coming up.

My father died ten days shy of his forty-ninth birthday—on Mom's forty-ninth birthday. Billy Martin declined to give Mike a day off—only "immediate family" rated that—but Brad Corbett flew Mike to Perryton in his private plane after the game. Mike and I will never forget Brad, the most giving man we've known among baseball executives.

I'm not claiming anything special about my dad and me. Everybody knows the way Texas dads love, cherish, and obey—even spoil—their "little girls." My father was like that, but it never showed until his last weeks. I hardly remember him ever saying he loved me until I went off to college. Yet I knew the depth of his feeling for me.

In one of the last of our long conversations on the seventh floor, Dad told me his only regret in dying at forty-eight, besides not being able to see his grandchildren grow up, was that he had never been very good about letting people know the good thoughts he had about them. He made me promise that if I *ever* had a good thought about anyone, I would not delay putting the thought into words.

At the end, he did something, even at death's door, about paying back what he believed he owed life. We found out about it posthumously.

When the cancer people told him he would not leave the hospital alive, he gave permission to make him a guinea pig for any experimental drug or treatment they might wish. He wanted to do this because at M. D. Anderson, one of the world's leading cancer-treatment centers, he was surrounded daily by young children with the same disease. Seeing them made him appreciate the forty-eight years God had given him. How could he resent the ones he would never see?

A few days after we buried Dad I was on a plane to Milwaukee for the 1975 All-Star Game. Mike had been selected by the fans for the American League team. I did not feel like going—after all, there would surely be other All-Star years—but I'm glad I did. Mike still wears his All-Star ring. He never made the team again.

I'm sure my dad would have wanted me to take that road trip with Mike.

Don't Burn Any Bridges

N o w that the "returns" are coming in, I would have to cast my final vote heavily in favor of Bradford G. Corbett. There were times I wasn't so sure. I've got to tell it all. But, like Bob Hope sings in that song, thanks for the memories.

If the Texas Rangers, under Martin, played a version of what six years later would be Billy-Ball, Mike and I played Brad-Ball. For three or four years it was a real roller-coaster.

The thing is that Mike and Brad were rookies together. That "vintage year" was also Brad's start. He bought the Rangers two days before the 1974 season began. He took Bob Short's dying franchise (dead last in 1973: won 57, lost 105, and 37 games out of first) and, under Billy, saw his Rangers come in second behind the world champion Oakland A's (won 84, lost 76, only 5 games out).

For a long time I just assumed Brad Corbett was a Texan. Maybe if I had known from the git-go that the big cigar and the western hat were a New York City boy's way of belonging, I would also have accepted those anything-is-possible days for what they were: fantasy.

I never put any of this together when Mike and I were livin' it up, and in the many conversations when Brad and Gunnie were with Mike and me (especially when he decided overnight at his fortieth birthday shindig after Mike's eighteen–home run 1977 season that Mike and I should join Gunnie and him on a junket to Europe). The temporary-high nature of things isn't exactly in the front of your mind when your boss offers you a ten-year big-bucks contract and a brand new car—*any* car you want. We just never came down those years.

Brad was brought up on Long Island, a place I've never been but that, I imagine, is about as much like the Bronx at 161st and River (Yankee Stadium) as Strongsville is to certain parts of Cleveland. Brad even had major league hopes. They ended about as deep in the minors (Fargo, North Dakota) as where Mike started.

He arrived in Texas—Fort Worth—in 1968. Two years later he was a millionaire. Except that it was happening all the time in Texas back then, I'd compare Brad's rise in his league to Mike's in his. He got himself a $300,000 government loan and Brad-Balled it into a fortune in the plastic-pipe and copper-tubing business.

At the time Brad was president of Robintech, Inc., he had eighteen plants in eight states. Of all his holdings, however, the one that touched Mike and me personally during those never-again Ranger years was his ownership of a Learjet. I have already told how Brad had Mike flown to Perryton after a night game so he could be at my dad's funeral. That was during our second season, a gesture straight from Brad's big heart. Sometimes, although Brad always meant what he said, he didn't always remember his promises. I imagine tycoons have a lot on their minds. Today's deal made over cocktails may be part of tomorrow's forgettery. Take, for instance, that fortieth birthday party at the Shady Oaks, a place of happy memories but also, at least once, the other kind.

This was just after our fourth season—Mike's last .300 year with Texas. Brad was holding court with us and Toby Harrah and his first wife, Pam. There was a way he and the cocktails had of having their effect—the two together—

but not enough so we weren't hanging on every word. There was ole Brad saying why didn't the six of us go over to Sarasota in his Learjet and check out Instructional League. Toby, Mike, and he could assess our rookie talent, and Gunnie, Pam, and I could get the off-season started right by lounging in the Florida sun.

"You know Brad" was a signal of consolation Mike and I often used after such talk. But it had been a long season, Mike had hit .305, I wasn't pregnant, and I figured either my mom, who had moved to Fort Worth after dad died, or Mike's mom would watch our two babies. I wasn't about to let Brad's latest offer go down the drain.

"O.K., *when?*" I blurted out.

Brad went for the little date calendar he kept in his suit pocket. "Can't go next week because I have to go to Europe."

I chimed right in on that, too. "Sounds *great.*"

"Do you want to go?"

I wasn't about to check my hearing. I said yes.

We moved to tables for dinner. Mike was at the same table but far away. I imagine he and Toby and Pam were enjoying their food. I had other thoughts. As if in answer to them, a sweet lady knelt down beside me. "I'm Frances, Brad's secretary," she said. "He wants to know if you and Mike can really go to Europe." I pretended not to be doubled-up with surprise. "I thought he was only kidding."

Later Brad asked if we had passports. This was a Thursday and he wanted us to be ready to go Monday. Fortunately, we four had gone to Japan two years before as representatives from the Rangers on a goodwill trip under religious sponsorship. We could be ready in three days. Brad eased everything including offering the family maid to watch Kim and Missy.

Mike was cautious. If the Harrahs would go, so would we. I said I was going no matter who went. Pam called next morning. She felt like they couldn't get ready that quickly. She didn't feel much like flying anyway. When Mike saw

I wasn't kidding about going alone if necessary, he agreed to go.

We didn't have to take Brad up on his offer of a babysitter. Mike's mom and dad, as they always did, came to the rescue. We met them halfway to Perryton with Kim and Missy. I packed quickly—what else is new?—and bought us some traveler's checks, which *was* new.

It was fabulous! Even though we Texans speak English like it is a foreign language and Tex-Mex was the closest to a nonnative tongue I had ever heard, I had the same experience as many other innocent Americans abroad the first time. Everybody speaks English, especially when you are traveling first-class. We flew to Zurich, then to Berlin. We rented a car and drove over the Autobahn, which I admit compares favorably to our Texas highways, which were the best I had seen. We flew home out of Paris on the Concorde —only three and a half hours in the air. Why, some drivers take that long to get from Amarillo to our place.

I have to tell you about Brad Corbett's generosity overseas, which in itself was as fabulous as at home, maybe more so. In Germany, he told Mike he should buy a Mercedes. When Mike said he couldn't afford a car like a Mercedes, Brad offered to get him one. We checked it out and learned that you could not buy a new car in Germany unless you had driven it beforehand. That didn't hold Brad up a second. We should pick out a Mercedes back in the states.

Brad may have meant the offer in fantasy land but we thought it would all be forgotten once we touched down in Dallas. We didn't have long to wait to find out once again that this was a man of his word. Two days after our return Brad phoned. Had we picked out a Mercedes? What were we waiting for? "And send me the bill."

Mike liked what he saw. Maybe I remembered something he had said after playing on Astroturf at the Dome: you feel you ought not to spit unless you can mop it up. That's the way I felt about owning a Mercedes. The idea of a young mom with two babies spitting up and dropping crackers all over the seat. I sort of lost interest. Our Chevy Impala was serving the purpose, wasn't it?

We had a real fuss. Mike always dreamed of owning a Mercedes. He didn't give up without a fight. But Brad wouldn't take no for an answer. We should go and pick "any car you want. Send me the bill." Mike suggested a Lincoln (I had an aunt who drove a turquoise Lincoln, which I remembered from when I was a kid). Like the Mercedes, it was too rich for my blood. Only ladies who had raised their kids and had them all through college drove Lincolns.

Mike doesn't get mad often but when he does—like on our honeymoon—he can be nasty. "If somebody tells you that you can get any car you want, you mean you're going to get a Toyota because it is good on gas?"

He wouldn't even take me with him to the Lincoln dealer in Arlington. He went with Bill Zeigler, the Rangers' trainer. They arrived in jeans and cowboy boots because they had been out riding horses. That dealer didn't give them the time of day. Guys looking like that couldn't possibly be serious customers.

That night Mike took me by the show window and pointed out a pale yellow model he thought I might like. It didn't take me long to decide I could live with it. Mike remembered the uppity Arlington salesmen. We drove to Corsicana and bought the identical model. About all I spent that day was the money to buy one of Corsicana's famous fruitcakes. The car never cost us a cent.

The Lincoln stayed with us long after we left the Rangers and Brad Corbett. We kept it in the garage at Strongsville Mike's first six years with Cleveland. During our seventh and last, a clubhouse boy wrapped it around a tree. That Lincoln died a hero. The police officer said that the three kids in the car would probably have been killed if they had been in a smaller car. It was the last big car Lincoln made.

I would like to have maybe a fender to display in my front yard in Perryton. Just to remember . . .

Brad sold the Rangers not long after we were traded. He never did bring Texas a pennant, although he did his best to buy us one. He was one of the new breed of baseball owner, which you can identify easy if I just mention the name George Steinbrenner. It used to be your owners would take a couple days off to welcome the players for spring training, shake hands with the rookies, and tell everybody this was the year. Then they would disappear into their family boxes and boardrooms. The Steinbrenners, Krocs, and Corbetts changed all that. Whether it's shipping or hamburgers or plastics, those kind of people want to be in on the action.

I remember late in what would be his last season with Brad—1978—Mike phoned me from Milwaukee. The Rangers had lost, 2–1, and were cleaning up when who should kick open the door of the clubhouse but Brad.

"At first he didn't say anything." Mike told me. "But he was breathing mighty heavy." Then, according to Mike, he started shrieking. He let 'em all have it. The team had no pride. If the guys weren't playing up to potential, it certainly wasn't because they weren't paid well. He said he'd go broke if he had to. "I'll fire till I'm dry," Mike quoted him as shouting.

Brad's had to have been one of the biggest payrolls in ball during Mike's last two seasons. Free agency—that is, putting yourself on the market to the highest bidder—was going clear through the roof in those days. Brad bought Bert Campaneris, Doyle Alexander, Richie Zisk, Doc Medich, Mike Jorgensen—all high-priced. He traded for some really big stars who had seen their best days—Al Oliver, Jon Matlock, Bobby Bonds.

"We were impressive—in the record books," Mike would tell me. "I guess we're impressing each other instead of the opposition." Mike felt especially bad he had only one season playing with Al Oliver, whom he considered the best hitter he ever played with. "I know for myself, as a matter of pride, I want to show someone from the National League — someone like Al Oliver — that I'm a good hitter, too."

It was really a bad scene, that 1978 season, especially after it got off so well. Two or three years after that Brad sold the team and may have saved his sanity.

I know we almost lost ours.

Of the baseball wives who answered the questionnaire we prepared once we knew we were going to do this book, no one was more down on ball than Patti Lake. Her husband, catcher Steve Lake, had reaped from the game nothing but serious and painful injuries. In her view, nothing compensated for eight years in the minors and a series of brief stops in the Big Show. Then Steve and Patti found themselves in the 1987 World Series. How "smelling the roses" just that once changed everything is told by Patti in the Appendix. Now I have to tell you about a time in our baseball life as God-awful as Patti's, a time of trying to cope and doubting myself as woman, wife, mother. When our accountant told me that, if nothing changed in 1987, our expenses would be ten times our income, I made myself think back to a certain autumn evening in Texas.

The night of the trade.

We had been in our first large house — thirty-four hundred square feet, right on Lake Arlington — for only a few months. It was the 1978 season, Mike's fifth with the Rangers. Although he had hit .300 or better three of those years, 1978 was an unfortunate season to hit less and make as many errors as he had ever made in his career. For only the second time in their seven years, the Rangers were challenging. They would win eighty-seven games, only to finish just behind Kansas City in the American League West.

To be doing so well, Brad Corbett had had to open up his purse strings. The team carried one of the heftier payrolls in ball.

Mike was struggling. I was six months pregnant. He was hitting around .250. I was the shape of things to come. Mike was the ghost of times past. We had had five managers the previous season, with Billy Hunter the holdover skipper. Hunter began pinch-hitting for Mike against left-handed pitchers. Nothing like it had happened before. But much worse than being hit for was being fielded for. Mike Jorgensen, who Mike never denied was a gold-glove first baseman, began to replace Mike at first in the late innings. To top everything off, about two weeks before the season ended, Mike sprained his ankle and was out for the rest of the season.

These were all firsts for him and all at once. Kim and I—I include my oldest daughter because she had been in the stroller as early as Mike's second season—were having our first, too. We would go to the final games that season and never once see Mike play. Then the trade rumblings became a roar—even before Mike was benched.

I never heard of a player—or any concerned wife—who prospered during trade rumors. On one of those nights when he was injured Mike sat in the stands with Kim and me. Within two innings, the fans' ridiculous comments drove him upstairs. He walked right up to Brad Corbett's box— they had that kind of a relationship anyway—and asked him right out: "Brad, am I going to be traded?"

Brad looked him straight in the eye. "I'd say at this point, it's about 70/30—70 you won't, 30 you will."

Later we learned that the deal had already been made. But I'm getting ahead.

After the season I went home to Perryton on a visit while Mike went to a convention in Atlanta on a promotion deal. Like I said, the birth of our third daughter, Pam, was less than three months away. The Yankees and Dodgers were playing in the World Series again. One day the phone rang. It was Grandma Gee Gee saying she had just heard on KEYE that Mike had been traded to the San Diego Padres.

It was a shocker. Any trade was bad enough, but to go to the other league was the worst. I've never been intimidated by anyone since Mr. Keller at Gastonia and I knew Mike would hate hearing the bad news like that. I phoned Dan O'Brien, Ranger president, but got his wife, Mary Ann. Dan was at a reunion—somewhere in New Jersey, if I remember right. Mary Ann gave me a number. I reached his hotel, left a message. He returned my call.

"Has Mike been traded?" I asked.

"Where did you hear that?" he replied. Didn't I know that nobody could make a trade until so many days after the World Series?

"Is Mike going to be traded?" I repeated the question. We'll always be grateful for the way Mr. O'Brien let us know without breaking his team's confidentiality: "I can't tell you anything, but I wouldn't be putting in a swimming pool in the backyard if I were you."

At least we had an inkling. It's the suddenness of trades that makes them hard. It's enough to drive a person nuts. I've known couples who had to read it in the paper.

Thank goodness, Mike's trade came during the off-season. Later, when he was traded back to the American League to Cleveland, we were two months into the 1979 season. That time Mike couldn't move fast enough. He was so glad to get off Ray Kroc's team.

Our first trade was official right after the World Series. That gave us some time, but it didn't make it any easier, not if you had been eating, drinking, breathing Texas Rangers for five years.

Now I come to the day we should always remember when we think things are the pits. It was October 24, 1978, a Saturday night. Frances had phoned Mike the day before. Brad wants you and Sharon to have dinner with him tomorrow night.

I heard Mike's reply. How could I forget it? "What is this, the Last Supper?" I cannot to this day believe Mike even said it. He knew he could joke with Brad's secretary and it would go no further. She asked, "Where would you like to go?"

"I think McDonald's would be appropriate." Mike answered.

If you check the Baseball Register, it will say that Mike Hargrove was traded October 25, with third-baseman Kurt Bevacqua and catcher Bill Fahey, for outfielder Oscar Gamble and catcher Dave Roberts "and cash estimated at $300,000." The Rangers got even more — $400,000. Eddie Robinson — he was Brad's general manager — traded Mike for a big wad of cash. Brad sure must have needed it.

We ended up having dinner at the Shady Oaks Country Club, the place I so envied our rookie season. While Mike and I knew what was coming, we figured we would be told in private.

We should have known better. It was only a couple of years earlier that Brad had taken us to Europe in his private plane — just to get away. On this night there were five business associates with us, all trying to sound natural talking baseball. It was awful. Finally Brad, not knowing what a can of worms he was opening up, said in an unnatural voice everybody could hear: "What would you say, Mike, if I told you we're thinking of making Eddie Robinson our hitting coach next season?"

"I didn't know there were two Eddie Robinsons," Mike said in that mock serious way he has sometimes.

"I mean *our* Eddie Robinson."

Mike wouldn't have said what he did if he wasn't sure he was no longer on the Rangers. As it was, he didn't even break stride. "I don't think there's a man on the team who will listen to a word he says."

If I had been smarter—if I had known then what I know now—I would have told Mike to cool it about Eddie Robinson. I've since learned you don't ever burn any bridges. Mike got along fine with everybody connected with the Rangers —except Eddie Robinson. He was a first baseman, too— with the White Sox and the A's in the 1950s—and Mike always thought Eddie didn't like him as a player.

But, to get back, Mike's reply killed all the questions and the phony camaraderie.

"Sharon," Brad leaned over and spoke in a whisper, "I need to talk to you."

"You don't need to talk to *me*. You need to talk to *Mike*."

"No, I need to talk to *you* because you're killing me."

I've heard some pretty macho guys say they can handle anything except a woman when she's crying. I was in tears by this time, and I wouldn't want anyone to think of Brad Corbett as macho. "You're killing *me*," I sobbed through the tears. "And you will never replace Mike Hargrove on this team," I heard myself saying.

"At least I'm not trading him to Siberia," Brad said.

The trade to San Diego was officially announced next day. The phone started ringing off the wall almost immediately. Like I say, Mike's never been much good at holding back his feelings. Something about seeing it in the Dallas newspapers opened up the floodgates.

Mike was nearly out of his mind. He felt betrayed. He felt like he had given the Rangers everything he had. The record will show that never once in the five years had Mike Hargrove gone on the disabled list. Not that he ever thought it was any big deal. Mike has always played hurt. There are players—superstars even—who ask out of the lineup every time they have an ache or pain. I could mention names, plenty of them.

We love Texas. For us that's where's it's all at. Arlington's not around the corner from Perryton, but at least our families could come in to see Mike play occasionally. In

Mom, whom everybody calls
Kackie, and me during the good
times in Arlington, Texas.

fact, after Dad died, Mom never went back to Perryton. She
has lived and worked in Fort Worth since Mike's second
year. We could meet for brunch any day we wanted.

When you're all agitated, whether it's in ball or anything
else, that is just the time you should back off. It's a hard
lesson. Randy Galloway of the *Dallas Morning News* has
been a big Mike Hargrove fan since he wrote that great column Mike's rookie year. When Randy asked him if he was
bitter about the trade, Mike let it all hang out. He let his
emotions take over. He told Randy that he had no bitter
feelings about anyone in the Ranger organization with one
exception: Eddie Robinson. The day after the announcement, it came out in the paper, and not just on the sports
page. It made page one.

Mike dreaded having to go in and face Eddie Robinson.
He told him he was sorry his words came out in the paper

Safe at Home

Our Homes Away from Home in Baseball

Perryton, Texas	Hometown
Alva, Oklahoma	College Baseball
Great Bend, Kansas	Semi-Pro
Liberal, Kansas	Semi-Pro
Geneva, New York	Rangers' Rookie Club
Plant City, Florida	Rangers' Minor-League Camp
Gastonia, North Carolina	Rangers' Class A
Sarasota, Florida	Rangers' Instructional
Pompano Beach, Florida	Rangers' Big-League Camp
Arlington, Texas	Texas Rangers
Yuma, Arizona	Padres' Big-League Camp
San Diego, California	San Diego Padres
Strongsville, Ohio	Cleveland Indians
Tucson, Arizona	Indians' Big-League Camp
Phoenix, Arizona	Athletics' Big-League Camp
Batavia, New York	Coach, Indians' Rookie Club
Kinston, North Carolina	Manager, Indians' Class A
Williamsport, Pennsylvania	Manager, Indians' Class AA
Perryton, Texas	Offseason Home

This list includes only the places where we have lived: eighteen cities, ten states, 1970–88. In our eighteen years together, Mike and I have made fifty-eight moves between these cities.

but that he wouldn't retract them. Why, he asked, had Eddie always had it in for Mike as a player? Eddie denied it. Basically, the Rangers needed the $400,000.

I think each of them had new respect for the other after that.

You never want to burn bridges. I knew that when I got to San Diego I wouldn't be talking about Texas and how the wives on the Rangers did things.

When we pulled out of Arlington, our spirits as heavy as the U-Haul trailer we hooked onto our Blazer, Pam was two and a half weeks old. It was early February, 1979. We had seven to ten days to drive to San Diego, get moved into the sight unseen condo we had just purchased, and backtrack three and a half hours to Yuma, Arizona, for spring training.

On the second day, I noticed Pam had a strange-looking bump inside her upper lip. It gave me a sick feeling, which turned to fear when I sat her up and noticed the same type of bump on her head. Half afraid of what I would find, I looked and felt around Pam's tiny body but found no more lumps. As we proceeded around Albuquerque toward Phoenix, the lumps grew larger. By the time we arrived in San Diego I was frantic. I feared the slightest knock would cause them to burst open.

We drove immediately to the ballpark and asked for the Padres' team doctor's name and address.

I remember the forms the nurse gave us as interminable — in fact, "terminal" may even have been going through my head. When you're trying to appear calm while contemplating the chances for survival of your three-week-old baby, it's not easy going through all those questions, especially when you barely remember the name of this new place that you and your family just pulled into.

When we finally brought Pam before the physician, the doctor to whom the Padres assigned us appeared to think he was there to talk baseball with Mike. My husband finally lost his patience, extremely rare for him: "Let's see to what we're here for. The baseball can come later."

The physician assured us that what we had located on our baby was commonplace: hemangioma, that is, accumulations of broken blood vessels. They can occur anywhere and are congenital lesions, small and closely packed capillaries that would be reabsorbed into Pam's system.

When might we expect them to disappear?

"Oh, routinely around the time the child reaches ten."

Was my beautiful baby girl going to have lumps for the next decade?

Pam's hemangioma, which I can spell only with the help of a medical dictionary, did indeed disappear within a few years. They were much simpler to diagnose and treat than first-trade withdrawal.

Everything seemed to be piling up. For one thing we had been training with the Rangers at Pompano Beach for four springs running. I'm not one ever to complain about geography, but I have to say it now. Coming from the Florida beaches at Pompano to the Arizona desert at Yuma was a letdown.

To begin with, we had a difficult time finding a place we could call home for the six weeks we would be there. There were the five of us — and Pam, less than a month old. People don't welcome you with open arms. Even Mom sometimes gets less than excited when we drop in.

Once again I was forgetting our slow starts in Geneva, Gastonia, and Arlington. Mike wasn't having a picnic, either. He had to begin again — prove himself all over — this time not only with a new team but in a new league. It may sound like that shouldn't be hard on a guy who had already played five years in the Big Show. Yet it's hard to put an "established pro" tag on any player. Maybe it's the player who pressures himself more than it is the new management and teammates.

Some of the pressure is to show your new team they didn't make a mistake trading for you and your old team that they did.

All players traded to the other league know they have to learn the pitchers all over again. Even the umpires' calls at the plate are slightly different. And Mike, who had done some D.H.-ing before he became a regular as well as during his last two seasons in Texas, couldn't help but be aware that the National League didn't have the D.H.

When Melissa, two years old, began to whine a lot and refuse to eat, I put that down to the posttrade blues. Ignoring her symptoms as long as I could, I finally decided it was time to get us a family doctor. Finding the right physician in a new town is no different for families in ball than it is for any other. We had been blessed in Texas with the services of the team doctor, B. J. Mycoskie. How I wanted to be able on a moment's notice to pick up the phone with my usual S.O.S.

Instead I called the Padre office in San Diego. Did they have a family physician available in Yuma? They were no help with their suggestion that I take Missy to the emergency room. Wonder how long it would have taken me to figure that out on my own.

It seems anywhere we have gone we have been blessed with an "instant long-distance family." Even in otherwise alien Yuma we found a wonderful neighbor on whom we were dependent and with whom I left Kim and Pam. I took Missy to the emergency room and waited two and a half hours as our problem kept getting topped by more urgent ones. Missy's lack of appetite, her slight fever, and general fussiness must not have sounded serious. In common with most mothers, I have an instinct about my children's state of being, and as we sat into the third hour, I lost my normal patience.

"How much longer?"

"Oh," said the receptionist, "I guess I had forgotten you were waiting."

I stayed cool, asked where the doctor's office was. As had happened with Pam and her lumps, there were forms to fill out before Missy was diagnosed—congestion—given a prescription or two, and I paid the bill.

Missy's condition worsened—especially on one side of her head. We weren't giving the medicine enough time. That was the doctor's response. Mother's instinct prevailed. I began to probe about in the nasal passages and, lo and behold, my tweezers brought out a ball of cotton. Normally, I would not leave cotton balls lying about. Then the answer came to me. With a newborn baby at home, you often have to dab the navel with alcohol to help the umbilical cord fall off. Missy had found that dabber and thrust it up her nose about three weeks earlier. It had found a home in her sinuses. Once I removed it, Missy never missed a beat. She practically ate us under the table that evening.

A few weeks later I found myself and our three little girls, along with Carla Fahey and her seven-week-old son, Scott, waving bravely to our hubbies as we prepared to face the long drive in the desert back to San Diego. In spring training the players are never allowed to leave camp with their families because there are always exhibition games en route.

Yuma to San Diego normally takes only three and a half hours. It can seem much longer with four kiddos. You leave the desert floor and climb nearly five thousand feet and then back down as you approach San Diego. At the peak, literally, the Blazer began to subside and hop meekly down the highway. Carla and I looked at each other. Mustn't alarm the kids. We pulled to the side of the road to figure out what to do. Two young men told us about an isolated gas station and suggested we press on, no matter what.

The Blazer got us there before yielding up all its fuel in a couple of gushes. With a lighted cigarette dangling from his lips, the attendant looked up from under the hood.

"You blew the fuel pump," he said.

Four hours later and $76 poorer, we pulled away to the accompaniment of the kids' refrain: "Make it keep hopping, Mommy!"

Minutes later, I spotted a sign from heaven: Food. Next exit.

Food has always rated near top priority, and the place where we stopped even served us a well-deserved glass of wine. Our high spirits were dampened when Carla discovered she was out of baby formula. This three-time mommy convinced the one-time mommy that Scott's chances were better with Pam's formula than with none.

It is amazing what a little food, a couple of good belly laughs, and a rest can do for the soul. We approached the

Interstate, which we knew would bring us into San Diego.

The capability of fate to dictate that misfortunes occur in spurts took over. Arriving at the condo we had occupied only two days before Yuma, I simply could not budge the garage door. I proceeded to pull, tug, and yank. Something had to give—me—flat on my backside and letting my laughter join that of Carla and the kids.

By this time it was quite dark, a fact that came home to us when the overhead lights didn't work. Our neighbors, the Thompsons, and I had exchanged hi's—and only that—a month ago when we had departed for spring training. I was desperate now, and Tommy Thompson certainly appeared not to mind when I awakened him and asked if we might borrow a lamp. It was he who noticed that the dead bolt on the garage hadn't been released. He unlocked the door and let us in.

Our husbands, understandably concerned, received our call with relief.

After the season opened, my newly found independence only slightly more reinforcing to such projects, I decided to take the children and visit Texas during Mike's first road trip.

My brother Benny had moved to Arlington with his family. Therefore, the three girls and I had a place to stay. I bragged to my sister-in-law Connie and to anyone else who would listen what a good baby Pam was. She confirmed my bragging—for the first night.

The usual explanations for what we hoped was temporary colic seemed to fit. She was slow to get over the flight from San Diego; her crib was different; her aunt and uncle, seeing her for the first time, were ministering to every whimper. Pam was simply spoiled.

One morning as Connie and I sat drinking coffee trying to recoup a sleepless night, she suggested I might try using distilled water to mix Pam's formula. Connie would go to

the store for it that very morning. No need, I said. I had
already thought of it—a change of water being salutary. I
had taken her distilled water from the pantry. Connie then
dropped a bomb. The stuff I assumed was distilled water
was her plant food.

I felt my temperature go up, my head get limp. I rushed
to the phone and instinctively called my old friend, Texas
Ranger medic Mycoskie. I didn't even have to look up the
number. Dr. Mike was out of town. His nurse suggested I
call Poison Control. After explaining in a torrent of words
what I had unwittingly done for the past five days, Poison
Control put me on hold. Had anyone calling P.C. in as hysterical a fashion ever been put on hold?

Looking back, I suspect that the delaying tactic was to
buy P.C. time to obtain the right advice. I had two courses.
I could take her to the Emergency Room at the hospital to
have her stomach pumped; but that would only eliminate
the most recent dose. Better, I was counseled, to force-feed
Pam—formula or water—as much as we could.

At times like the one just described I am often overcome
with uncontrollable laughter, a kind of hysteria. I am certain the voice on the phone would like to have added, "Yes,
force-feed and preferably *without* fertilizer."

In my defense, I would like to be able to say that I broke
into laughter *after* Poison Control convinced me there
would be no danger once the fertilizer was purged from
Pam's system. I can't say that. Mike was not amused either.

"You're just like your mother," he said. "You both go
around someone else's house like a chicken with its head
cut off helping yourselves to anything."

I should have been mad—or wise—enough to vow nothing like this carelessness would happen again. I knew better.

Who thinks to ask questions when holding something
routine-looking like a bottle of clear liquid marked "distilled
water"?

I wish this had been the end of it. A few days later I received a call from Tommy and Eileen Thompson in San Diego asking how Pam was. They had just read in the newspaper that I had fed her fertilizer. I could only guess that Mike had told one of the players all about it and a reporter, overhearing the story, had added an item to "Padre Notes." Thanks, Mr. Media. Now how do I face the Padre fans sitting by the wives' section?

"Isn't she the one who fed her kid fertilizer?"

The guidebook I read when we were traded says San Diego is often known as the Cradle of California Civilization. That title will always be inseparable in my mind from cradle stories. You've heard about the illnesses that beset my two babies within a few weeks of our arrival.

There's one more cradle yarn that would head up any catalog of horrors I might compile to this point.

Somehow we never got over being lonely for Texas. I was overjoyed when a dear friend, Claire Smith, came out from Arlington for a visit. I stowed the girls in the car, Pam in her car seat up front and Missy and Kim in the back, and off we sped to the airport.

I would be a perfect hostess. We would have lunch at a San Diego pierside restaurant. The girls had their instructions, well practiced, about getting out, opening the door for our passenger, and taking Claire's hand. I got out after the others to feed the meter. Missy, in a spurt of overkill, slammed my door for me. The only problem was that the doors were locked with the keys—and Pam—inside.

There are frequently hotter days in the Metroplex summers between Dallas and Fort Worth than balmy San Diego ever experiences, but in my mind at that moment, as I became aware of our predicament, was how intolerably hot it must be for my baby inside. My car was the kind that had locks with no knobs. There was no way the coat hanger trick could be worked.

I hailed the first police car. He came over. How long had

the baby been locked inside? I had an impulse to shout, "Three hours at least!" but my words came out more accurately: five to ten minutes. Pam had begun to cry.

The policeman suggested breaking out the back windshield. That would be fine as long as he could assure me the broken glass would not touch Pam.

Did I know exactly where the keys were?

Occasionally in my life an ordered ritual recurs. I keep keys in the same place in the diaper bag, always. This is a must for moms: to be able to place their hands in the bag, grab the keys while balancing baby on their hip. The officer took the coat hanger provided by a passerby and successfully lassoed the keys out of the diaper bag.

As he was pulling them up, the officer saw the inscription on the chain: "Mike Hargrove, No. 21 San Diego Padres." "Are you Mike Hargrove's wife?" "Yes, sir," I said, looking him full in the eyes. "and I'll have your badge if this makes the paper!"

Who can say when, even in San Diego, things cannot go any lower? I began having chats with God. Their gist went something like this:

"Hey, God, you've gotten us traded from Texas, where we were happy to San Diego, where we're miserable. You've messed up my friendships in Texas and put me through all this trouble out here. What have You got to say for Yourself?"

Not even God would dignify that kind of self-pity with an answer. I began to rethink the questions.

"But God, what have you really taken away from us? Texas, although it's awful big, is a hunk of geography. God, you've kept us all together. My family is intact. Your transplanting us out here is one of Your blessings in disguise. I've got everything that matters."

I determined to straighten out my act. I was experiencing a weight problem for the first time in my adult life. I started a diet. I took long walks. With three babies, I knew

Why is this man smiling? This must have been
the only time during his brief stay
with the San Diego Padres in April–June, 1979.

there was a limit to how fashionable I could be among some
of the California fashion-conscious wives. I was already
wilting under the strain of mixing formulas, changing dia-
pers, getting the kiddos ready—Kim, four, almost on her
own; Missy, two, on a leash—my hip; and Pam, four months,
in the stroller. I was change-resistant.

As it turned out, the shape-up-or-ship-out problem would
be settled for me.

By June, a third through the season, I was beginning to
make friends among the San Diego wives. Two volunteered
to help me fix up the condo—new curtains and wallpaper.
I was getting adjusted, but Mike's problems kept mounting.

Always a slow starter at the wire, Mike never found a
groove in San Diego. He was in and out of the lineup—
mostly out: a new experience. Never before had we had any
problem talking baseball. He had taught me well; I had
come to love the game. Now he would come home after
night games, a living version of the old story every baseball wife has heard about the slugger who goes hitless and
whose wife greets him: "What happened out there today,

honey?" The player-husband snaps: "You take care of the cooking. I'll take care of the hitting."

For the first time in ball Mike seemed to be going well —too well—beyond our unstated vows never to let the game take over our lives.

"When I leave the ballyard, I want to leave the game behind too. If anything changes, you'll be the first to hear."

And I was, too. Two months into the season Mike called me from the stadium: "Sharon, guess what? We've just been traded!"

What the Baseball Card Doesn't Show

In 1985, when Mike declared free agency and it looked as if his playing days with the Indians were over, we decided to keep the big house in Strongsville. We rented to Tony and Iris Bernazard (Tony played second base), who had three boys and needed the room as much as we did. On our way to Batavia from Perryton in July, we stopped in Cleveland for a chat with Danny O'Brien. We also made a stop in Strongsville to pick up some things. I had a chance to talk to Iris, who told me one of the best stories I've heard on baseball dads and their kids.

Ebony, their oldest, then just past three, was watching TV with a friend. The Indians were on the tube and Tony came to bat.

"There's your dad," said Ebony's little friend.

"No," said Ebony, "that's not my dad. That's Tony Bernazard."

For me, Iris's story not only illustrates the old Bible adage about wisdom coming from the mouths of children but says something about how our kids can misperceive their dads as being different from the guys they see on the field or on the Topps bubblegum cards.

Our Andy was just about the same age as Ebony Bernazard, but I cannot imagine him sitting long enough to watch a game on TV, not even one with his dad in it. Andy got to see his dad in uniform real close in those tiny Class-A yards. I can't imagine him confusing the guy who coached at third as other than the same guy, wearing civvies, who drove us home afterward.

To our kids it is nothing special for their dad to be involved with professional baseball. They grew up seeing him on TV or his picture in the paper. I have never discussed with them anything about how they should react to seeing their father perform every night. I imagine they felt like it was something all dads did. They didn't see the novelty of it until they began school and the other kids let them know their dad was a big deal.

It isn't that way in Perryton, where, unless their parents make the connection for them, none of the kids are old enough to remember Mike's Texas Ranger days.

It was different for Kim and Missy. Kim went through almost all of elementary school in Strongsville during Mike's seven years with the Indians; Missy went up to 2nd grade. We couldn't even go to Back-to-School Night without being hounded by the other kids. It was nice but hard on the girls, especially Kim, who wanted us to see her art work and writing samples and couldn't figure out what the big fuss was all about.

The time I remember being the hardest for Kim was in 1981, Mike's third year in Cleveland,

I think Mike secretly envied Missy's speed on the bases.
She stole more bases during the kids' game on Family Day
than Mike did his entire career.
Photograph courtesy Janet Macoska.

when the players went on strike. She came home
from school near tears saying someone had told
her that their dad said Kim's dad was already
making too much money and yet wouldn't even
go to work because he wasn't making enough.
Missy, who is twenty-one months younger and
wanted to help, chimed in that her dad didn't
work anyway; he just played baseball.

We have never, not when he was earning a veteran player's salary, or now, when his pay is less
than most of their friends' dads', told the kids
what Mike makes. We feel they would not understand why it has fluctuated so much. We won't
be surprised if Kim asks us one of these days

about something she has seen in the paper. So far that hasn't happened.

If anyone, it is their dad who understandably has had some trouble making the connection between his roles as ballplayer and parent. He missed Andy starting kindergarten; he had to be away heading up Instructional League in Sarasota. Kim has started school sports, and he'll probably miss most of her basketball season. I don't know of any wives in baseball who, if they have kids, don't list their husbands' absenteeism at or near the top of their grievances. Some of us pretend to shrug it off with a resounding "That's baseball!"

Having their dads playing ball is not all bad, not by a long shot. During his playing days Mike got to see his kids growing up with a closeup look that few working fathers get. I was reminded of this by something Katharine Hepburn said recently in a TV interview. She was saying how raising children the way she would have wanted would have been out of the question and be an actress, too, and she can't imagine how actors can be good fathers, their working hours being what they are. I can sure see what she means, but I have to say that ballplayers, who keep the same hours as theater people, get to stay home mornings and afternoons. They see their kids, especially when they are little, on a day-to-day basis, which is out of the question for working dads.

Mike is very close to our kids and affectionate (even with Andy, who prefers not to kiss Dad when other players are around). Mike took Kim on a road trip to Kansas City when she was eight. That night, while she was taking a bath, he rolled back the covers and placed a new nightgown on

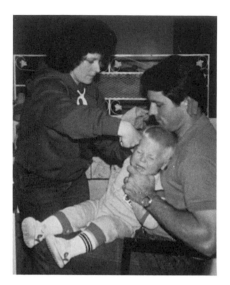

That's Mike restraining Andy
as the shears are applied for
Andy's first haircut.

her pillow. To this day Kim talks about her road trip with Dad.

Mike has been with me at the birth of all four. He was tender and caring at such times, extremely proud of each baby and always the first to get his hands on them (something I always thought was terribly unfair). He will do just about anything for his kids, but he is hard on them, too, when it comes to the real nitty gritty. He wants very much for someone in this world besides us to think they are neat.

Natalie Prusak, our babysitter throughout most of the Cleveland years, came down from Strongsville to visit us in Kinston. What struck her, seeing Mike at Kinston in a family situation she never saw in Ohio, because he was at the

ballpark any time she was with our kids, was
how glad he would be for a rainy day so he could
be with us.

Remembering Mike as her hometown Indians'
first baseman who happened also to be a neighbor, Natalie was struck by the way he could be
so detached from baseball around the house that
it always surprised her when Mike would put
away the paperback he was reading—usually
American historical or military fiction—and get
ready to head for the ballyard.

"Was Mike like this when he was playing?"
Natalie asked me one day.

I think I replied that I couldn't imagine a husband in baseball who brought less of the game
home with him. But if that was my answer, it
was an oversimplification.

Sports may be one of the very few jobs you
can't leave at the office. Baseball is a fishbowl,
and the Mike Hargroves are inside. An o-for-4
night—getting the horse-collar—can be as bad as
it would have been if I had flunked that certifi-
cation exam they gave all of us Texas teachers
in 1986.

The fan looks at the box score in the morning. If that fan really follows the team, he may
notice a lineup change or a player having a good
or bad day at bat or in the field or on the pitching mound. What doesn't show in the box score
is the ebb and flow of a career. The agonies of
the player who is also her husband don't get by
a caring wife. She lives with them every game.
She may worry more when stony silence or some
put-down remark greets her question about how
the game went that night. It happened during
the bad weeks in San Diego, before the Cleveland

Indians rescued us, and it happened at the end in Cleveland, when Mike could see Pat Corrales was phasing him out.

You try at times like that not to let him leave for the game without a hug and an "I love you"— both truly meant—and the same when he comes home. If you don't pay attention—if by your indifference to the way his game is going you tell him you don't care—you are likely to lose a bigger game.

Late in the 1987 season, Cleveland sent us a bonus draftee who had signed late. The can tied to his butt said he often showed up late for the games, missed buses, and was a disruptive force in the clubhouse. After this kid reached the wall of a building far beyond the left field fence in his first batting drill, Mike took him aside and told him how glad the Kinston team was to have a guy who could hit those four hundred-foot taters. He also explained the ground rules for belonging to the team: he would never be criticized for mechanical errors or errors of aggression or for taking a swinging third strike in the clutch. But Mike would play him only as long as he showed up on time for practice, hustled, and listened to his coaches.

We learned our lessons early in the smaller *and* the larger games. We had it out early and by Gastonia each knew the other could be relied on. I'm grateful, too, to Mike's mom, who taught him long before we got married what a woman needs.

Mike is an easy-going person. Rarely have I heard him use strong language at home, even though I know he's no gosh-darn-it man in the locker room. After all, his first manager in ball was Billy Martin.

Just before the end of the first half in our league, Kinston lost a doubleheader, each game by one run in eleven innings. That put us out of the running. When Mike got home, I could see he was fuming.

"Did you have a clubhouse meeting?"

"Dammit, I sure did. I told them if they played like that, before they knew it the second half would be gone."

Mike doesn't often raise his voice at home. I had only heard "dammit" in extreme situations. Had he really chewed the team out?

"Sharon, dammit, it's hard to get your point across saying 'gosh darn it.'"

Judging from the reports I've heard from his coaches and players, Mike has no trouble communicating—on the field. Off the field, it is often harder to deal with relationships. Mike is a 6-foot, 205-pound hunk of man. Grown men don't cry. I've been hearing that in and out of sports all my life. Give or take one of those candid shots from the losing team's locker room, athletes don't cry. In all our years of marriage I've seen Mike's eyes fill many times: at the birth of each of the kids, at my dad's funeral, when accepting the Good Guy Award after his final season with the Indians, in the parking lot in Phoenix when we first saw each other after the A's said he didn't fit into their plans and we realized his playing career had ended.

But I've seen those tears unwillingly overflow, too. Most of such times have been over family matters.

Like the day a neurologist in Amarillo confirmed that Kim's fainting spell in church had actually been a seizure and that she was epileptic.

Like the day we were told that Pam, fourteen months old, would be in a body cast the next six to eight months to correct a congenitally dislocated hip.

Like the day the doctors wheeled Missy, age eight, off to surgery to rebreak a bone in her arm and put her elbow back in place after a trampoline fall.

Like the day he rushed home from a rain-delayed game only to find Kim in her First Communion dress, staring blankly at the clock, and realized she had just missed her Communion.

Maybe Mike's biggest heartbreak to date links in with my biggest. Our dads. Cancer and alcoholism have this in common: they creep up. If you fight them early, there's a chance.

My dad learned about his malignancy too late. With Dudley we had more time.

Just about the time Mike made it to the majors, his dad began drinking for the first time in his life. Our folks were whispering about it when we came home to Perryton after our vintage year. But my own father's death was so recent—my first pregnancy so all-consuming—that Dudley's problem slipped to the back burner.

The next year Mike made the American League All-Star team, we traveled a lot, and eventually bought a large house on Lake Arlington. We were spending less and less time in Perryton. The trades to San Diego and Cleveland got us farther and farther from our roots. When, spring of 1980, we went to Tucson, Arizona, with the Indians, we heard of a rehab facility nearby. We did our best to persuade Dudley to enroll. But he was a contract pumper (oil wells) and couldn't or wouldn't leave his job.

Kim's First Communion, Strongsville, Ohio.
That's her younger sister, Missy, at left.
A long (real) rain delay that Sunday
had caused Mike to miss the actual Mass.

I've already written at great length the reasons
we bought the spread just outside of Perryton.
What I didn't mention was Mike's notion that
he could do his dad's job for him in the off-season
while Dudley was getting help. Either because
of pride or a feeling he could lick his problem
alone, Dudley refused Mike's offer. For about five
years we watched his drinking get worse. It was
awful, being near Dudley most of the off-season
months. Somebody had to put it on the line for
him.

I nominated myself and voted myself in. Once
I had studied rehab places, prices, and availability
—once I felt certain our families' offer was the
kind he could not refuse—I went to Dudley after
Mass one Sunday shortly after the final season
in Cleveland—1985. We had arranged for him to
check in at a certain place the next day. Would
he go? At first he held out, but when I made it

Safe at Home

clear that all of us who loved him expected him to say yes, he did.

That afternoon all the Hargroves of Perryton, including his eight grandchildren, greeted Dudley and his decision with open arms.

"He's going to go," I said as Dudley and I entered the family room.

Everybody ran to him. Mike's mom, beginning to cry in large sobbing gasps, embraced him, the oldest of the grandchildren grabbing for his legs. I have always considered baseball a family matter. Here was another.

Dudley entered a six-week program of therapy and has remained sober since.

6

Indian Rescue

JUNE 14, 1979 is one of the few dates that are not birthdays that I'll remember. It was the day when Mike called me from the San Diego clubhouse to tell me we had been traded again. At that moment, baseball stopped being a game.

I have already said how little stock I place in hindsight. Still, when I look back on the shock of the trade to Cleveland, I have to say that even though five of Mike's seven years with the Indians would be his happiest in ball; even though I detected a happy throb beyond the familiar rasp in his voice when he announced we were leaving downer San Diego and Mike's happiness has always come first with me; and even though I now know that it was in Cleveland where I came to terms with myself as a baseball wife, mother, and person — in spite of all the good things that would be happening to the Hargroves throughout the first half of the 1980s, I cannot at this late date think of June 14, 1979, as anything but as it looked to me then: hideous.

Except for letting out a loud "shee-yit!" when he announced that we were headed for Cleveland, I tried not to put a damper on Mike's joy. I played my favorite role of the sacrificing wife. Hadn't I been telling myself and anyone who would listen that I could not be happy unless Mike was happy? Here was another chance to practice what I had been preaching. I tried to sound as bubbly as ever, but after we rang off I started bawling.

I'm glad the girls were too young to notice anything different about their mom. I would have to pull myself together. Mike had been given the news just before suiting up for that night's game. He would be home any minute. The Indians had already ticketed him for a 7 o'clock flight in the morning, although traded players are supposed to get three days to report to their new teams. We had never been involved in a trade during the season, but I wasn't so dumb not to know that the Indians wanted Mike in their lineup right away just as the Padres wanted Paul Dade, the outfielder for whom Mike was traded, in uniform, too.

When you're feeling real sorry for yourself, nothing breaks through. I looked at the bright wallpaper that I, with the help of a couple of the Padre wives, had just hung. Now it was that very wall the fates of baseball had me up against. Sometimes my emotions give in to meanness.

If baseball can do this, well—dammit—baseball will have to pay for it. Ever since Geneva—hell, ever since we lived on the golf course at school—I had done everything myself. Now the professionals would have to do it for me. Strictly business. I sat myself down, made up a simple chart. There were Points A, B, and C. A was San Diego, where we were leaving; B was Cleveland, where we were going; and C was Perryton where I had to go, if only temporarily, to deposit the girls.

The pilgrim spirit overcame me. I phoned Mayflower. The little Texas gal from the sticks who paid parking fees at Arlington Stadium before she learned she could get a permit to the "preferred" section would now bill someone—Padres or Indians—for every inconvenience. The bloom was off.

This message is being brought to you courtesy of major league baseball.

Every time I get down on ball, something or, more often,

someone turns up to renew my spirits. This time it was my brother Ben and his wife, Connie. Benny and I have always been like peas in a pod because he stayed behind in seventh grade and we went through the last six years of school together. It turned out they were driving their Toyota pickup and camper to San Diego to see Mike in action for the Padres. With Connie and their two-year-old Bryan sleeping behind, Benny was pushing hard through Arizona when he heard the news of Mike's trade on the car radio. This was around 2:00 A.M. Benny turned the vehicle 180 degrees. They were headed back to Texas until he heard a rap on the cab window.

Next thing you know he had done another 180-degree turn. "We're going on to California," Connie must have ordered. "Sharon will need help."

I did indeed. Thanks to Connie and Benny, we were ready the day after they arrived. Our little caravan made it to Perryton in four days. I left the kids with Mike's folks and took a plane to Detroit.

By that time Mike had been with the Indians two weeks and was playing every game. André Thornton, who would later be named team captain, was one of the game's sluggers. He was also the Indians' first baseman. Mike had been moved to left field, a position he had played frequently in Texas.

I arrived in Detroit just as Mike was about to board the bus for Tiger Stadium. He gave me a kiss and the number of a room where I was to meet four of the Cleveland wives to go to the game.

Now I've been on teams where my introduction to a wife was a bonus car (as with Janet Sundberg at Plant City) or a striking hairdo (as with one of the gals on the Padres). My first inkling about the wives in Cleveland in 1979 was more like a whiff. I had never smelled marijuana before, but three of those four Indian wives were smoking away with something that wasn't tobacco. More in inexperience than indignation, I turned down the joint one of them offered.

I knew there would be changes in Cleveland. Pot wouldn't be one of them.

Cleveland, like New York, Detroit, and Chicago, was one of those big cities many small-town persons like me just assume are unfit to live in. How I learned differently is a big part of this chapter's story. Mike, who still hadn't learned not to tip his delivery, told a *Plain Dealer* sportswriter, right from the git-go, that Cleveland was one of his least-favorite cities to visit as a player. He had the sense to qualify that judgment by saying that visiting players only see downtown at 12 o'clock at night, and that's never real pretty.

The way Mike caught fire almost immediately, it was easy for Indian fans to forget his newcomer remarks about their city. No fans had (in fact, *have*) suffered longer than those in our new city. No pennant since 1954 and lots of last-place teams and, according to Terry Pluto and Jeffrey Neuman in *A Baseball Winter: The Off-Season Life of the Summer Game* (Macmillan, 1986, p. 201), "a bewildering series of strategic shifts . . . that make fans wonder if anyone in the [Cleveland] front office has any idea of how to build a winner."

Almost from the time he arrived on June 15, which was the trading deadline, until the end of the 1979 season, he was just about the hottest hitter in the American League. He batted .325—as it turned out, the highest he would ever hit—and had ten homers and fifty-six runs batted in. Mike likes to point out that in his last seventy games, after getting himself adjusted to Cleveland, playing left field instead of first base, and hitting first in the lineup, he batted .375, with an on-base percentage of .474, which was the highest in the American League.

Not only was Mike back in familiar surroundings, where he knew the opposing pitchers and ballyards, but it seemed half the Indian lineup was composed of guys he had played with on the Rangers. After the God-awful 1978 season, Eddie Robinson not only had sent Mike packing to San Diego but had run a player shuttle with Gabe Paul of Cleveland. Mike's old pal Toby Harrah had been traded off Texas for a big Cleveland favorite, Buddy Bell (Toby also had a great year with the Indians, but Buddy had an even greater one in Texas; for a time it looked as if Toby's luck had run out, but he soon caught on); Len Barker, who two years later would pitch the perfect game I wrote about earlier, and outfielder Bobby Bonds had come over the previous October; and even before that the Rangers had unloaded the troubled David Clyde, the Houston high-school pitching phenom.

More important, according to Mike, was the presence of two other old friends who were coaches on the Indians. Joe Nossek and Dave Duncan were in charge of the hitters and pitchers, respectively. Mike has tried to explain to me his hitting problem, which got straightened out in Cleveland. You see, almost nobody on San Diego had ever seen Mike play in the American League. Mike credits Gene Tenace, a catcher-first baseman who had signed with the Padres as a free agent after Charley Finley broke up his championship Oakland team in 1976, with convincing him that anyone who had hit big-league pitching for five years would hit well again. Joe and Dave got Mike to hold his hands much lower on the bat. Later, after Joe and Dave left the Indians and new manager Dave García brought on Tommy McCraw, it was Tommy who helped Mike with the mental aspects.

As far as *my* mental aspects were concerned that first half-season in Cleveland, they remained on a scary hold until the schedule ran out, which couldn't be a day too soon. I had done another fast round-tripper to Perryton for the kids, moved briefly into rental housing in Cleveland, and come to the realization that in another year Kim would be in school and things would be getting tougher. It was good that fall and winter to be back in Arlington in the lake house, where Mike and I would be seeing a lot of Peg and Rich Donnelly and Janet and Jim Sundberg, who were lucky enough to live there year round.

One warming discovery of the 1979 part-season was that in a real baseball town like Cleveland, and unlike the Metroplex, where the Dallas Cowboys are king and baseball hadn't yet caught on, there were and are fans who eat, drink, and sleep Indian baseball. A group of rooters cottoned to Mike from the start. They christened themselves "Hargrove Howlers," brought inscribed banners to the game, and kept in touch with us all winter. One of them, Amy Knott, arranged to be in Strongsville the following April to help me unpack the van.

We had bought, without more than a quick look-see, a split-level house in suburban Cleveland, not more than twenty-five miles from Municipal Stadium. Mike had gone to Tucson and spring training alone. I had planned to go with him, but we discovered that Pam, fourteen and a half months old, had a dislocated hip. While in traction she developed an ear infection whose pain ruled out any sleep. I stayed in Arlington to nurse my youngest daughter through the crisis.

One thing Mike's absence has taught me — something you come to appreciate about baseball — is never to panic. I came awful close while Mike was playing a boys' game out in the cactus country. When camp broke, the Indians headed for the season opener in Anaheim. I headed for Cleveland. By then we had the big van, and I did my first long-range packing (Tucson to Cleveland is about fifteen hundred miles). I lay my "corseted" baby on the floor of the vehicle, with the five-year-old Kim sitting guard and the three-year-old Missy in her car seat up front with me. It took us five days.

When I walked for the first time into the house that I

had seen for less than an hour (and that would be our base-ball home for the next seven years), I felt as though I was in a fishbowl. It didn't have drape one. I thought we had made too quick a decision. It just didn't seem like home.

Trouble comes in twos, as I would quickly learn.

Amy Knott, the member of the Howlers who had ar-ranged to help me get set up in Strongsville, stayed the first night. We watched the Indians play the Angels on a bor-rowed TV. The girls, stir-crazy after being in the van for five days, unlimbered by jumping into a beanbag chair. Kim fell.

"I think I broke my arm," she said, trying to sound brave.

I left our Howler pal with Missy and Pam—thank God for her—and rushed Kim to the hospital. The arm was bro-ken in two places.

It was 2:00 in the morning. I wanted to cry. Naturally, I lost my way coming back from the hospital. We didn't have a phone in the house and I was afraid to stop that late at a pay phone anyway. Finally I found my way back to the house.

The next night I met Mike at the airport. He saw Pam in her body cast. Missy had a black eye from a collision. And then he saw Kim's arm in a cast, too.

"Sharon," he said, "what are you doing to these kids?"

It's the way I'm carved, I guess. I saw the humor in Mike's remark. Everything was fine. It didn't even matter that we had no drapes.

If 1978 and 1979 were our two worst years in ball, 1980 and 1981 (until the big strike of June–July, 1981, that is) were, all things considered, our best. Or maybe, just this once, I'm thinking *me* more than *we*. I finally got my act together.

In Texas I had started to learn not to be intimidated by Gucci bags while I was carrying lunchboxes on one arm, Kim on the other, and Missy in the stroller. By the time we were in our first full season in Cleveland, Kim and Missy were walking hand-in-hand and Pam was in the stroller. By

1983, Mike's last real good season with the Indians, there were four lunchboxes and three pretty girls hanging on for dear life and Andy, eighteen months old, occupying the stroller. Maybe it wasn't such a bad thing for the Hargroves, domestically, that we didn't get many big crowds in Municipal Stadium those years.

Now I'm not saying that, take away my four kids, I wouldn't have dolled up, too. What gradually happened in the Cleveland years was that I began accepting myself as well as the daily ritual. It became a matter of good faith for our entourage to reach our seats before the national anthem. I don't remember Mike, who would never do such a thing, blowing us kisses during the "Star-Spangled Banner," but he has always wanted to spot us from the dugout while the flag's being raised.

We are talking about seven hours every home game when you log in half an hour to get to the yard from Strongsville, another hour at least for Mike to shower and join us, and another hour, at night, to get home.

By the time we would pull into the driveway, Mike would have been at the stadium since about 3 o'clock; the whole gang of us had been thinking baseball from no later than 6 o'clock. By midnight, the earliest I could expect to have the kids in bed, Mike and I had just about all of ball we could take. Even a little ball went an awful long way when the going got tough the last two years.

But that old law of diminishing returns was years away on the last day of the 1979 season, Fan Appreciation Day. It proved to be Hargrove Appreciation Day. The public-address announcer, without mentioning the name, began running down vital statistics, topped by a .325 season average, which could have belonged to no other Cleveland player, finishing up with: ". . . . And for your play, Mike, here's the key to a brand new Monte Carlo, just a token of Cleveland's regard for you."

Fan Appreciation Day, Cleveland 1979, was particularly

satisfying as the unexpected highlight of a season that had started with a .192 batting average in fifty-two forgettable games at San Diego. In two segments of a single season Mike had "achieved" his lowest and highest career averages.

Mike has said that Reggie Jackson, having retired after the 1987 season, will go into the Hall of Fame at Coopers-town his first eligible year—1992. Mike says "Mr. October" merits the honor—563 homeruns, including 5 in the 1977 World Series and 100 or more with three different teams. Reggie has also struck out more than any other player in baseball history and finished his long career with a lower lifetime batting average than any outfielder now enshrined at Cooperstown—around .260.

Mike's fondest claim for himself is at an opposite end of the hitting spectrum. He would like to be remembered as as good a man at "putting the ball in play" as there has been—what the baseball people call a contact hitter. Mike hit only eighty homeruns in twelve seasons, but through the 1982 season he had the highest on-base average of any player in the major leagues. With bases on balls added to base hits, his well-over-.400 average for his first nine years was tops among active players in baseball).

What Mike will be remembered for, if anything, is some-thing that never appeared in a box score or in a record book. Although we are at chapter 6 and heading for the home-stretch of our career, I have barely mentioned the batting ritual Mike trademarked that made him notorious with some fans and writers and the butt for many a humorous quip by such baseball announcers as NBC's Joe Garagiola and Baltimore's Chuck Thompson.

In brief, Mike used to dig a hole in the batter's box, tug at every piece of his uniform, and—given four at-bats a game—might be considered to have caused a slowdown of every game he ever played in.

Hal Lebovitz, who was sports editor of the *Plain Dealer* when we arrived in Cleveland and who took Mike to his heart in much the same way Randy Galloway did in Texas, told me the first time he interviewed me that Mike's "schtick" (as Hal referred to it) irritated him no end when he played for the Rangers. Maybe that's why, now that Mike was on Cleveland, Lebovitz wrote the definitive account.

"Before each pitch, Hargrove goes through more motions than a burlesque dancer with the itch. His ritual involves 14 different motions, from pushing down a thumb pad on his left hand, to grabbing his belt in the middle of the back, to pushing his helmet down tight. Then he is ready. The routine never changes."

I never told Hal that once Mike received a roll of toilet paper with an unsigned note to "clean up your ____." I would rather remember the daddy sitting behind me telling his son, "See that guy and how he really gets ready for every pitch. And don't think he isn't psyching the pitcher too when he delays things that way."

Which is the real point.

There are some funny and not-so-funny stories about how pitchers came to hate Mike's slowdown tactics.

During his last year in the American League, fellow Texan Nolan Ryan yelled at Mike so loud that you could hear it from the wives' section, "For God's sake, hurry up!" Nolan is not known for such outbursts. One irritated pitcher threw the ball over Mike's head when he eventually got in the batter's box.

While going through his "adjustments," Mike leans his bat against the inside of a thigh. While Mike was playing for the Rangers, Tom Buskey, pitching for the Indians, threw the ball between Mike's legs and hit the bat. Ron Pruitt, who was catching for the Indians, told Mike, "That's been Buskey's lifelong ambition."

I do know that Mike started the ritual in the minor leagues. Anybody who has ever hit their funny bone knows the numb feeling you get. That was happening to Mike's left thumb every time he hit the ball at Gastonia in 1973.

Instead of checking with the team doctor or trainer (since lower minor league teams are not afforded that luxury), Mike devised a shock-absorbing pad made of gauze and taped it to the base of his thumb. He made those gauze pads for twelve years in the majors.

The pad would fly off occasionally, so before each pitch he would screw it down tight. You know how you turn on the ignition key. Everything starts with that. Everything started with that thumb pad. He would find himself thinking about the pad instead of concentrating on the pitch. All those mannerisms came to get his concentration on the pitcher back. I guess he kept adding to his repertoire.

It was while we were going good in Cleveland that a Toronto sportswriter dubbed him the Only Human Rain Delay.

The early years in Cleveland, which were also the start of the new decade, are inseparable in my mind from the short strike of late May, 1980, and the real thing of June, 1981, which lasted seven weeks and a day, "wiping out 713 games — a third of the 1981 schedule. The financial losses, it has been estimated, exceeded $70 million in ticket, concession, and broadcast revenues and $28 million in player salaries. The damage inflicted upon the status of baseball in the affections and attention and loyalty of the fans can never be measured" (Roger Angell, "The Silence," *Late Innings: A Baseball Companion* [Simon and Schuster, 1982], pp. 382–83).

The strike lasted so long that, for the only time in baseball history, the season was divided into two halves. Unfortunately, the Indians were out of it both halves.

When Judy Sammons of the *Plain Dealer* interviewed me for an Indian wife's reaction to the first threatened strike, I recalled the time when we were in spring training with the Rangers — it was 1977 or 1978 — and the owners locked out the players for several days. Brad Corbett called all the

This is the "human rain delay" sequence
Mike became famous—or infamous—for.

families together and offered interim compensation to tide
over anyone who was short of cash. It was a sort of joke.
When Brad mock announced that there were greenbacks
galore under the table, I made a mock scramble for them.

The real strike was not funny. I could not imagine having Mike home during the season, remembering how antsy
he always acted just before spring training. I told Judy that
I was behind the walkout but what I was really thinking
was how many of us wives could cope with our husbands'
idleness. We had just moved into the split-level in Strongsville. There should be plenty to keep Mike busy.

Kim, having just turned six, was playing on a T-ball team.
It was almost like the ballplaying never stopped when Mike
and I would go watch her play. If it hadn't been for the strike,
I guess Mike would never have seen Kim play. Often we
would go from Kim's game to see Mike play for an indus-
trial league team. Then, after Mike's game was over, we
would go to the Dairy Queen for ice cream.

This ritual drove opposing pitchers to distraction.
Photograph by Ron Kuntz, courtesy Cleveland Plain Dealer.

The first time was something we hadn't had in years: all of us together like any other young family enjoying the summer—Mike ordered himself a particularly big cup of ice cream. He had just started to eat when a bunch of Little League kids, fresh from a victory, came hoopin' and hollerin' by our table. One of the kids recognized Mike and asked for his autograph. No need to describe what happened next. It was like those tumbleweeds latching onto our fence in Texas. Mike never took another bite.

As I said, at least during our years, baseball was bigger in Cleveland than in Arlington. Strongsville is barely a half hour, unless traffic is heavy, from the stadium, which is in downtown Cleveland. When kids found out where we lived, they would get their parents to drive right up to our door. Talk about snowballing.

Often players are criticized for not doing for others. But think of it. If Boy Scout Troop 37 asks Mike Hargrove to come and speak to them—and if he accepts—bear in mind there are hundreds of Boy Scout troops all over Cleveland and vicinity—which ones do you say yes to and which ones do you say no to?

It is hard, too, for the players to do charity work. Greg Luzinski used to foot a big bill to make it possible for thousands of disadvantaged kids to see baseball at the Vet in Philadelphia. The work of Ted Williams and Yaz and other Boston Red Sox stars for the Jimmy Fund is legendary. Since 1977, the Dave Winfield Foundation has brought thousands of disadvantaged kids to games, enabled them to meet players, and provided them with health education and care.

Sometimes it's easier to donate money than time. The only time they really have to devote to charity projects is during the off-season. Many players do not live in the cities where they play. When we played with the Rangers, we lived in Arlington all year round. We could be at many off-season functions. There were a lot of charity basketball games until a player would get hurt and have his next season—occasionally, a whole career—messed up.

This is a good time to quote from one of Mike's Cleveland contracts, under "Prohibited Activities":

> The player agrees that he will not, without the prior written consent of the Club, participate in any of the following activities: auto, boat, or motorcycle riding; piloting of aircraft, parachuting or skydiving; boxing, wrestling, karate; judo, football, basketball; softball; tug of war; weight lifting (unless properly prescribed or supervised by an authorized representative of the Club); skiing; hockey; and/or any other sport or activity not specifically listed above, which involves apparent and significant risk of personal injury or death.

I might note that the players' union contract requires that players have an off day at least every nineteen days. For most of the other eighteen—that is, for playing dates,

Mike's schedule was fuller than just a couple of hours before, then the game, and an hour after. I think few readers
have any idea how crowded a day baseball makes. On a home
date (that's about half the time during the season),

Mike gets up around 10:00 A.M.; has a cup of coffee;
   reads the paper.
Eats his big meal—lunch—around 12:30.
Leaves for the stadium no later than 2:00 P.M.;
   30-minute drive.
Skill drills, extra batting, etc., begin around 3:30.
Home team takes batting practice; visiting team takes
   batting practice.
Team meetings, esp. pitchers, catchers, coaches, on
   how to pitch to opponents.
Home team takes infield drill; visiting team takes in-
   field drill.
Grounds crew readies the field 30 minutes before game.
Game time (7:30 P.M. in Cleveland).
Mike leaves locker room one and a half hours after
   game.
Arrive home around midnight, with all four kids up
   and wide awake.
Hungry Mike, who has not had anything to eat for
   twelve hours; fix Mike dinner.
Try to get four kids to bed and to sleep, anytime from
   midnight to 2:00 A.M.
Mike watches TV (late-late movie or talk show, mostly).
I take bath, fall asleep on couch.
Mike wakes me about 3:00 or 3:30 A.M. to go to bed.

When Kim started school our second fall in Strongsville
and Missy a year later, my morning schedule changed dras-
tically. I would have to be up to get them off early. Fortunately, I'm a sound sleeper who can drop off, wake up to
see the kids off, and drop off again. As a rule, I did not take
the kids to the games on school nights (that's how come

I missed Len Barker's perfect game). I would sometimes get Natalie or another girl to babysit and go alone. Usually, during the week, I would stay home with the kids, wait up for Mike, and still get up with the girls.

Mike would not see the kids during the week when school was on. He would be in bed when they got up and off to the yard before they got home. They were in bed by the time he got home. When you consider Mike was on the road half the time, he may have seen his kids about four days a month. These four days would be the two weekends the Indians were home.

It was no surprise that the absentee-dad aspect of ball dominated the downer side of my wives' survey (Chapter 8).

How our kids have stayed in school—and in baseball, too—is a story in itself.

Kim started first grade when she was six, and that was only two months before our youngest, Andy, was born—fall, 1981. That was when we decided to stay in one place all year. We picked a tough winter to make that decision.

Winter 1981–1982 brought Cleveland a record snowfall—upwards of one hundred inches. In the Panhandle, we get some snow, but it doesn't stay on the ground long. At any rate, we were more antsy that February in Strongsville than we had ever been in Texas for Gabe Paul's annual letter announcing the start of spring training in sunny Tucson. There was only one hitch. The principal at Kim's school told us we could not legally take her with us.

There's an Ohio law that says unless the child is enrolled in another public school within two weeks of her withdrawal from the first, she would be counted as absent. Kim stood to lose the whole year. In that case, I decided, we just won't withdraw her. Strongsville was cooperative. They gave Kim a grace period of fourteen school days before they began counting her absent. We obtained her work assignments from her teacher in Strongsville and got her a tutor in Tucson. Her record showed thirty days absent, but her performance didn't suffer. Technically, she had been absent two months. We had passed our trial year.

For the next few years—1982–1985—the logistics were even more complicated. Kim—and then Missy—would start the school year in Strongsville; then transfer after the season—in October—to Perryton until spring training; study with tutors in Tucson in February and March; and return in April to the teacher and class they had been with in September.

I simply could not see any other way of keeping us intact as a family through spring training, the 162-game schedule, the off-season.

One of the last things Gabe Paul, Indian president for nineteen years, ever said to me was that he marveled at how long I had refused to allow baseball to separate us as a family. When, in 1985 we finally did separate for the last days of the season, so the girls could begin school at Perryton, it was Gabe who added, "and baseball never did; *school* did!"

Texas will always be our spiritual home; we hoped we'd be Rangers forever. But Mike's best years as a player were his first four with the Cleveland Indians. He won the Player of the Year award two of those years. Of course, these prizes were voted by the media, and it is possible his popularity with the writers and TV people had something to do with it. The award he appreciated most was the Golden Tomahawk he won in 1980, because the players did the voting.

After the strike-bound 1981 half-season, Mike was moved back to his familiar first-base position, where he blossomed as one of the better defensive players at that position. In the second year of our six-year contract—1981—Mike was, except for Bert Blyleven, the highest-paid Indian. He also received about as fine a tribute from his manager (Dave Gar-

Here's how we looked in 1983 in Cleveland,
on our way to a game. Clockwise, starting
with our oldest, Kim, we are Pam, me, Andy,
and Missy, about to board our van.

cía) as a player can get. Dave told Hal Lebovitz on the eve
of the walkout that he figured Mike would go home to Texas
to get a job playing semipro.

He would have, too, except that he found a slow-pitch
team (Atlantic Tool & Die) in Cleveland. García's words
are ones I often thought about when Mike's career was wind-
ing down: "Here is a very unusual fellow. Naturally, everyone likes to get paid, but Hargrove isn't in this game es-
sentially for the money. He just loves playing baseball and
you pay him $50, $50,000 or even nothing, he's gonna give
you everything he has no matter what. You don't find too
many around like him."

Mike earned $330,000 in 1981, strike and all, which is pea-
nuts compared to salaries now but was very satisfying for
us, heading into our thirties and with four kids. The six-
year contract, which Mike would play out, was worth about
$2 million through the 1985 season. Big money on the bar-
relhead has been the ruin of many a career. Not for Mike.
"All the contract means is that we now have a bank account

worth keeping track of." That's the way he put it to Hal Lebovitz.

As you might guess, the feeling between Mike and his manager from the end of 1979 until near the end of 1983, when Dave García was fired, was close. Despite his usual slow Aprils and early Mays, Mike knew Dave would play him through slumps.

"You're my boy," Dave would tell him opening day. "You'll be in there somewhere — every day." From his arrival on the Indian scene in mid-1979 until early June of 1981, Mike played in 271 straight games, which is modest compared, say, to Cal Ripken, who played in his one thousandth early in 1988, but indicative of stamina and determination.

You will hear no sad songs from Mike about his last two seasons. Nor will this book sing them. As early as spring training, 1984, which as I've said is the time all of us wives prefer, Mike told me that he realized he no longer figured in the Cleveland Indians' future. By the end of May he was certain that he was like a spare part of his car, valuable only if there was a breakdown somewhere.

For the first time in his life in ball, Mike asked to be traded. If you're looking for symptoms showing that the fun is going out of the game, that's one of the most noticeable. "If the Indians are committed to going with younger players, then I should be traded," he told a *Sporting News* correspondent in early June.

Pat Corrales, in his first full year replacing Dave García, converted a twenty-six-year-old outfielder–third baseman named Pat Tabler into a first baseman and handed him Mike's job in March.

Throughout the season, Mike became the odd man out in Corrales' shuffling of younger players in an effort to juice up the weak-hitting Indians. It did some good, I guess. The Indians won 75 games of the 162 and finished out of last place — they were sixth in the seven-team American League East — for one of the few times in recent history.

Pat Tabler, Mike's successor at first base, made a name for himself on the Indians before being traded to Kansas City in early 1988. Mike says his record hitting with the bases loaded may be one of the best ever. Rather than try to describe in detail Mike's final season, I remember one story that will both put the cap on 1985 and symbolize the way we've come to regard the game.

We were packing our Strongsville place after the season and getting ready to rejoin our kids in Perryton. We would be renting the house to the Tony Bernazards. Because the kitchen was packed, our neighbor Marge Molnar invited me over for breakfast. Mike was still asleep at the house. I spotted this big article, the lead story on the sports page, about Pat Tabler. I knew Mike would want the paper to read while he was having breakfast. I had this feeling that he might not get beyond the Tabler story.

I decided to do something you have to do in ball when you would really like a crying towel. I borrowed Marge's highlighter pencil and highlighted the whole article on the man who had taken Mike's job. I placed the paper next to Mike on the bed.

When he joined us for breakfast, Mike was laughing himself half to death.

Sometimes that's the way things go. You have to laugh to keep from crying.

We Over Me

It's too late in the game now to do anything about it, but you may have noticed that most of this book has been pitched into the first-person plural pronoun. *We* were traded, *we* signed a multiyear contract, *we* took the girls out of one school and put them in another, *we* are hoping to make it back to the majors. This whole unreal world of ball self-destructs pretty quickly if

We took a Caribbean cruise
for our tenth anniversary, winter,
1980. Here I am, all dolled up
for the captain's reception.

couples don't slug it out as a team—we and us
and our over I and me and my.

Mike and I don't talk about we-ness much. It's
there all the time, though. Sometimes it has been
downright embarrassing, especially when Mike
downgrades himself and puts me on a pedestal
where I can never feel comfortable.

Sports Illustrated did a feature story on Mike
midway through his second year. He was getting
pretty well established by then. The writer, Larry
Keith, had a quote I wished Mike had not given
out: "I'm a lazy person, basically, and it's only
through my wife that I've learned to push myself." He pretty much said the same thing in 1987

to Hal Lebovitz, a columnist for several Ohio newspapers.

Now Mike couldn't have played for Billy Martin if he was lazy. He's an easy-going guy with an open nature that got him into trouble occasionally. If you're Reggie Jackson or the Boz—if you're *on* all the time—a backup person—a wife, say—might be extra baggage. Not every athlete can be a superstar with mouth to match. Poor Roger Maris—while he was hitting those sixty-one taters in 1961, his hair was also falling out. He needed all the backup he could get. I'm sure, as it has been so often with me and Mike, Mrs. Maris knew what was happening but couldn't do anything about it.

Some of us really like being first and foremost somebody's something. I'm like that. Ever since I can remember I have been known as G. K. and Kackie Rupprecht's daughter, Al and Benny's sister, Mike's girlfriend. Why should I have a problem being Mike Hargrove's wife?

There's a song—a poem, really—that says it all:

> It must have been cold there in my shadow,
> to never have sunlight on your face.
> You've been content to let me shine,
> you always walked the step behind . . .
> I can fly higher than an eagle,
> 'cause you are the wind beneath my wings.*

All I want is to be a tribute to each somebody's something. It has never bothered me that I have

*("The Wind beneath My Wings," by Gary Morris, words by Larry Henley & Jeff Silbar, 1981, 1983, Warner House of Music/Warner Bros. Gold Music Corp.)

always been identified through someone else. (Well, maybe just a tad when I'm asked, "Are you Mike Hargrove's mom?") It has, in fact, helped me. When I was in school, it helped me to meet people: "This is Al's little sister." Everybody liked Al, so they gave me a chance. When I went to college, it helped too. At Abilene, that first year of college, I was Al's sister again; at Alva, I was Benny's sister or Mike's fiancée.

Being somebody's something all my life has made it easier for me to meet people wherever ball has taken us. I feel sorry sometimes for women who have to make moves and have no way of meeting people. Another someone's something: Kim's, Missy's, Pam's, Andy's mom. They are the someone's somethings I love to hear during the off-season.

Everyone has identity in people they love. Sometimes that identity does good things for others we don't even see. I once helped raise $21,000 for a children's hospital in Cleveland, but I couldn't have raised a cent if I wasn't Mike Hargrove's wife.

It's a privilege, really, that I'm trying to live up to. I hate to see wives who expect special treatment. I've seen wives push their way through lines, be rude to ushers. I can't stand that.

The one time I did try to use Mike's name was with Neiman-Marcus. They were having a two-for-one sale on haircuts. I tried to squeeze in at the last moment. The guy in charge stopped me. "Let me just leave my name and I will go ahead with my friends here and if there is an opening, then I will take it." He said that would be o.k. and what was my name. I told him. He said it

Every year the Cleveland Indians provided uniforms
for moms and kids and held a Saturday family game
before a regular one. I got a chance to do
my "human rain delay" imitation of Mike at the plate,

sounded familiar. "Well," I said, "my husband does
play for the Texas Rangers." "No," he said, "it's the
'Sharon.' Have I ever cut your hair before?"

I always wanted Mike to play long enough so
that I would be considered a veteran's wife. I
dreamed that somebody's wife would look up to
me like I looked up to Kathy Jenkins and the late
Blanche Perry.

It hasn't worked out that way. Even though I
was older than the wife of Mike's manager—Pat
Corrales—his last year, I have rarely felt like a
vet's wife. I've never quite been able to figure out
why. Even in Cleveland after all those years it
was mostly because I knew the ropes that some
of the girls looked to me.

There is a larger question called "image." I really had to come back to the minor leagues to
be comfortable being myself. I knew from the git-

And we got to pose together
on the big diamond. That was 1982,
I think.

go that I could never fit the mold of the baseball
wife, TV-lens image. I tried to look my best and
be on my good behavior. It was only later in *my*
career that I learned I could not "play the role"
unless the role was me.

Mike has always told me what attracted him
to me back in seventh grade was that I was always in the gym playing basketball, screaming,
laughing, having a good time.

It is not my idea of a good time and being myself to come to the ballpark in high heels, carrying a Gucci bag with my needlepoint in my lap.
I prefer jeans (not necessarily designer), comfy
shoes, with a bag of popcorn nearby.

147

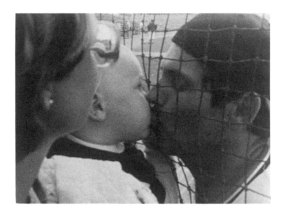

Mike and I have many pleasant memories
of spring training with the Indians at Tucson.
This was April, 1982, Andy "netting" a kiss.

Popcorn reminds me of our four kids. They
deserve a break, too. They come to almost every
home game with Mom. Maybe not always because they want to but because Mom thinks it's
important for them to know what their father
does for a living. But don't look for them to be
on their best behavior every game, sitting with
folded hands in their Osh Kosh outfits.

The View(point) from a Wife's Section

IN 1985, Mike's final season, we made $450,000, which may just prove to be the peak annual income in our lifetime. There were times when my simple mind could not grasp those numbers. I would hear me talking to myself: "Hey, Sharon, Mike makes more every two weeks than most people make in a whole year!"

That $450,000 was something Glenn Konet, our management adviser, called our gross annual worth. I think the choice of "gross" is perfect in more than one sense.

I am just glad that Mike and I never saw even one of those bimonthly checks eleven of our twelve years on the field. I might have been lulled into forgetting we were in a 50 percent tax bracket; that our management group takes 10 percent off the top; that for eight of those years we paid city taxes in Cleveland *and* Strongsville, not to mention that nine states with American League franchises taxed us; and that most of those years we were meeting hefty mortgage payments on at least two houses.

For the playing years, except the first, a Cleveland-based consultancy named International Management Group (IMG) took charge of our financial affairs. When they took over our finances, our yearly profile was covered on two typewritten pages. By 1985 the profile was bound in a notebook and totaled forty-six pages. IMG, despite a dramatic drop in "new" money, still pretty much tells Mike and me what to do. The only difference is that IMG does not receive our bimonthly checks. We went from a 50 percent tax bracket to a 0 percent one. Mike went from $45-a-day meal money in 1985 with Cleveland to $11-a-day with Kinston. A burger at the Comfort Inn at Peninsula, Virginia, on the other hand, cost somewhat less than a burger at the Sheraton Towers in Boston.

Since 1985 we have been playing another game besides ball. We have tried our best to live on our earnings rather than requesting "allowances" from IMG. It hasn't been easy. When the going gets tough, I just think of Kathy Jenkins, the wife of Fergie, the Rangers' highest-paid player, who turned me down on going to the show because she didn't want to go over her monthly budget.

Now I've got to backtrack just a bit. I haven't written much about Mike's salaries—and our expenses—over the years. At the start of our married life, only I was paying tuition and expenses at Northwestern State. As a scholarship athlete, Mike had pretty much a free ride. When we house-sat on the golf course, it was fun at the beginning, working on the place that was our first home together. To this day, though, I do not know what we lived on other than love. I'm sure Dad pitched in from time to time with sums close to what he would have been out if his daughter had to live in the dorm.

This I know. We had no steady income until 1972, when Mike signed with the Texas Rangers. Mike got the $2,000 bonus I referred to, and we thought we were flush with prosperity. We had no trouble living on rookie pay of $500 a month at Geneva. After all, Jane DiAngelo only charged us $15 a week for the attic apartment, and the only other expenses were food and gasoline. We left Geneva with the same Texas wardrobe we had arrived in.

When we moved up to Gastonia, the retroactive hike Mr. Keller allowed us at midseason from $650 to $750 enabled us to move into a real apartment complex and we gave ourselves the luxury of air conditioning and a $30 electric bill, which was big money in those days and which really upset Mike until I pointed out that it was worth $1 a day to have a cool place to live, a refrigerator that worked, and adequate lighting.

In Kinston our electric bill was $115 ($3.50 a day) for the same services but with four more customers. Inflation is especially dramatic when you move back, after fifteen years, to where you started. I really don't know how couples with children can make it in the low minors. We were already with the Rangers—with IMG overseeing us—when Kim was born (March 18, 1975).

After his vintage rookie year, Mike was invited to participate in an ABC television annual sports extravaganza called Superstars. Two by-products of that occasion were noteworthy—one immediate, the other almost immediate and certainly long range. The immediate one was that Mike glimpsed in the gathering of athletes one of his all-time idols, John Havlicek of the Boston Celtics. Mike thought he had a good-sized hand until he shook hands with John, who greeted him in words Mike has committed to memory: "Good to meet you, Mike. You had a great year." The long-range benefit is that we signed on with International Management Group.

That was after the 1974 season. From that day until this no one else has ever helped us with our financial planning. IMG charges a commission of 10 percent of your total salary. They assign you an agent, take care of your tax returns (his last year Mike would have had to do nine different tax forms), and build an investment portfolio.

Like I said, we never saw a paycheck. Rangers, Padres,

and Indians mailed our checks directly to IMG. They in turn put so much in our personal account each month, an amount mutually agreed upon as the figure we should live within. It has never been easy to ask for more money even though it was ours.

IMG handles the insurance needs of our family of six. They even file each claim, saving me hours. They have done so well that in the process of moving over fifty times since 1975 we have never received a forwarded bill that was overdue.

They never make investments without consulting us. Once Mike acted on a tip, and we lost our investment. IMG was able by investment to scale down our losses. They protect us from all the people—the honest ones and the vultures alike—who would like us to go into business with them ("Mike, if you'll put up the cash, I'll run the business"). They are a sort of cushion for us to bounce off ideas. Mostly, our ideas are not so hot.

I have known companies and agents who have really lost some megabucks for their clients. I see this even in the minors. What these "agents" try to do is jump on board the best prospects and line them up for later delivery.

The good ones deserve every penny of commission they make. When we were traded to San Diego, we still had three years on our Texas contract. All of a sudden we were out 12 percent of that contract just by playing in California. Then, traded same season to Cleveland, we had to pay Ohio state tax, too. In short, you need help.

Still, I think agents should have to be certified by the commissioner.

I have a t-shirt that says "I can't be overdrawn. . . . I still have *checks.*"

The only things I can truly say I have accomplished in the money game include learning to trade one first-class airfare for two coach tickets so Mike (if he really loves me) can take me along. Mike didn't like to see me clipping coupons while traveling first class anyway; talking a saleslady down on a rug in Neiman-Marcus; learning the truth of something Patty Blyleven said to me when Bert joined Mike and the Rangers in 1976: "Just give them that plastic card and they will give you anything you want!" A true (but costly) lesson.

My failures to play by the rules of the money game have been numerous.

One year in the off-season the Perryton post office phoned. A check had bounced. Not that I had never overdrawn. It was just that I knew we had money in the account, because Mike and I had only been home a few days. My error was clear as soon as I looked on the back of the check: "No account at this bank." Yes, of course. We were banking that year in nearby Booker. I had written twenty-one checks on a bank I didn't have a penny in.

The P.O. charged me $10. They also gave me our first registered letter since the one from Billy Martin inviting Mike to the Ranger camp. It was from the grocer. I left the P.O. knowing my multiplication tables well enough to figure I would soon be $210 out of pocket. I practically covered Perryton picking up checks.

If this had happened in Cleveland, I would surely have been turned over to the court. At the Christmas party given by the Booker bank, I was presented a giant-sized check so that I wouldn't make another error. I used it to buy some furniture, and the store sent it to the bank, which honored it.

Nobody denies I can tell a bargain when I see it. Only sometimes the bargain is a moving object.

I saved newspapers for years in our garage at Strongsville in anticipation of a windfall. Don't let anybody tell you ballplayers don't read the paper—at least two a day during the Cleveland years. When it came time after the season to move back to Texas, Mike strongly suggested I should get rid of the papers, a fire hazard. A neighbor showed me a coupon with the address of someone who offered to buy old newspapers.

Without any help from Mike, I loaded the papers until they filled the van and headed for Cleveland, where I was also to speak at a ladies' luncheon. I dolled up for the speech — dress instead of slacks, high heels instead of loafers. The paper outlet was in a crummy part of the city, but I went anyway. A voice on the intercom instructed me to drive into a weighing station, then to unload the papers. I was more in favor of somebody else unloading those piles, but there were no volunteers. I began tossing the stacks out of the van. Overworked, underpaid, and angry, I heard the same voice: "Lady in the van. You are unloading in the wrong place. Newspapers go in the southeast corner of the lot."

I had no compass but I reloaded and found the southeast corner. It took forever to unload again. I tried not to hear the comment of a man who dropped maybe a week's worth from his luggage compartment without giving me a hand with my summer's accumulation: "Lady, did you really drive all the way from Texas to sell those newspapers?"

At the cashier's cage, I was handed less than $5. It cost me $4 to have my dress dry-cleaned to get the newsprint out of it.

Just before another move — this one to Perryton after we finally sold the Arlington place — I took three grocery bags full of Mike's favorite paperback reading — western and military history and fiction — to a swap store. After sorting them out according to instructions, I was handed a slip of paper on which the figure $26 was written. Unfortunately, that was the amount of credit the store was giving me to buy more books.

One winter I heard about a guy who was trying to sell a truckload of firewood. He preferred selling all six cords to one person. How lucky for me. Mike being at the bank working, I got in touch with the wood seller. He came by the house but without the wood. His truck was in the shop. He would sell me six cords at $70 each. I gave him the $420 in anticipation of delivery next morning. I am still waiting.

One night in midwinter, Mike turned on the jets as high as they would go. When I asked him what he thought he was doing, he answered that he was burning up all the firewood I had bought.

When the National Football League players went on strike and with the court ruling in favor of baseball's free agents who, so the ruling goes, were victimized by a collective boycott by the owners, it is anybody's guess how much longer the two main professional sports in this country can continue without pricing themselves out of the market.

At the beginning of this book, I said that three off-the-field matters had determined, if not *what* my husband did on the field, at least *where* he did it, how long he did it, and at what price.

These were the baseball draft, multiyear contracts, and free agency. I discussed the draft as it affected Mike's start in ball, but I never did get around to the other two.

Ted Turner, the owner of the Atlanta Braves, "was in on the start of this free agent madness in 1975, signing Andy Messersmith to the original free agent contract" (Pluto and Neuman, *A Baseball Winter*, p. 76). To be a free agent is exactly what the term says. The veteran player, either unhappy or underpaid, or both, under his current contract, opts, after meeting certain longevity stipulations, to place himself on the open market. He waits for offers and accepts the one that is most satisfactory for him. The ruling on Messersmith removed forever baseball's exemption from antitrust laws, which, in effect, could bind a player forever to the team that originally signed him.

Until the 1986 season, million-dollar contracts were being offered almost routinely to free agents. In 1987, according to the ruling that went against them, the owners were in cahoots with one another not to sign any free agents. The unsigned players who declared free agency were prohibited from playing with their old teams until May—well after the start of the season.

Mike, his long-term contract with the Indians fulfilled, declared free agency after the 1985 season. It not only didn't bring any offers, it had a lot to do with ending Mike's career at that point. The owners retaliated at the start of the 1986 season by gaining the right to reduce their rosters from twenty-five to twenty-four players. Mike was Oakland's twenty-fifth man that spring and was released.

Anyone who says Mike and I would find it hard to be objective about free agency has a point. I will be content with making two points: (1) Actors, entertainers, TV news anchorpeople, etc., make baseball salaries look like peanuts. I don't hear anyone complaining about that. No one is forcing fans to pay crazy amounts to be entertained. It is their choice. If people are willing to pay out-of-sight prices to see professional sports, they have to realize the owners are making big money at their expense. Owners have to pay the entertainers—the players—and the entertainers/players are going to take every penny they can get their hands on. I like to put it this way: "You would too/If it could happen to you." (2) Some fans don't realize how brief a time the athlete has. Few remember that one pitch can end a career; one accident can bring a halt to the money. They have to make what they can while they can.

We always liked the security of long-term contracts. Sure, it bothered Mike (and other full-timers) to sit on the bench next to a guy who pinch-hit maybe once a week and made double your salary. You might call that the George Foster Syndrome. George never did much for the New York Mets even though, at the time of his signing as a free agent, he became just about the highest-salaried player in the game.

Then there's the Wayne Garland Formula. Wayne signed a ten-year multimillion-dollar contract with the Indians about the time Mike came to Cleveland. Wayne never came back from rotator-cuff surgery his first year under the contract. Although he pitched hardly at all in the 1980s, he was still drawing a salary from the Indians through the 1987 season.

Don't forget the Oscar Gamble Windfall, either. When Oscar was granted free agency in 1977, he actually signed for about $300,000 more than his agent had anticipated. Before the agent could say a word in negotiations, the club's general manager said in effect, "I can tell you right now I'm not paying you more than X dollars a year"—a figure higher than the agent had planned to ask. A year later he was traded to Texas in the deal that sent Mike to San Diego.

Not all players are in the game for the money. Mike once said he would like to form a different kind of all-star team: one made up of guys who can make the bunt and hit behind the runner; who agree to be sent down temporarily in the interests of filling a hole in the lineup; who keep the team loose in the field and the clubhouse but never play lawyer there.

Renegotiations stink and should never be part of any game. They are a sort of hindsight thing, too. If a player signed a contract, he did it thinking it was a good one. Then down the road he comes in with a demand to rethink the original. Did you ever hear of a player who, after a bad season, asked the club to renegotiate downward?

The contract Player A signed in good faith today becomes the gross underpayment tomorrow when Player B, who lucked into a Wayne Garland deal, is getting more and doing less. Tough. Teams do not ask players to renegotiate when their poor play is protected by the long-term contract.

I'm sure Player A would be shocked to be asked to give up what he had already agreed upon.

One of *my* greatest thrills in baseball was being in Boston when the Red Sox said goodbye to Carl Yastrzemski in 1983, after twenty-three years. He was forty-four and had played all his games, upwards of thirty-five hundred, in Boston. It's discouraging to think there aren't going to be any more one-team careers like Yaz's or Mickey Mantle's, Bob Feller's, Hank Aaron's, Ted Williams', Jackie Robinson's.

Whatever trades don't take care of, free agency will.

I first heard "franchise" applied to a single player our first year, 1972. It was applied to pitcher Steve Carlton. Steve, the sports pages said, was the Franchise, and no wonder. In his first year with Philadelphia, he won twenty-seven games, which was more than half the number the Phillies won that year. For the next thirteen years he *was* the franchise. Since 1984, and now in his forties, Carlton has been kicking around with many teams, a baseball freak.

Yaz went out the right way; Steve, the wrong. The Kansas City Royals signed several of their franchise players, including George Brett and Frank White, to lifetime contracts. That was a great move for the fans of Kansas City. Hardly anybody thinks of them anymore.

The first trade is the hardest. If the player is happy where he is, it must be like divorce without mutual consent. I hope I never find out for myself, but friends who have gone through divorce always talk about the overwhelming sense of failure. You've been discarded. Like none of the good things in the relationship matter any more.

In ball, it's like telling you the team doesn't need you, or at least not enough not to need somebody else more.

That season of 1974 there were 504 women married to major league baseball players. There were approximately 740 children who made up player families. Cleveland, the

Mike and I with our three preschoolers
during Mike's fourth season with the Cleveland Indians (1983).
Mike is holding the baby, Andy.
Missy, 5, and Pam, 3, are in front of me.

team we ended up with after a short stop in San Diego, was third in all baseball in number of players' children: 37. The Hargroves would add 4, passing the Phillies for second place behind Houston's 42.

That season four hundred major leaguers—husbands and fathers among them—were involved in player trans actions, according to the baseball commissioner's office. None of these included free agents who played out their contracts.

There are no statistics that cover the number of friends you won't be seeing again.

The reason for the trade can make a big difference. So can the city that will be the new home. It is one thing if the traded player knows his stats are so outstanding as to make him the key man. It's another if the traded player reads that he was "thrown in" like one final bag to fill the dumpster.

At best, being traded is like some low form of flattery.
At worst, it's the end of a dream.
You will always hear, "The trade benefits both teams."

"The Athlete's Losing Game"

I have known a lot of gals to get messed up in
this game. There are booby traps every step of
the way. Typically, we marry young athletes who
are attractive hunks of manhood. If these attractive hunks are successful, they can easily grow
further and further apart from us. The guy is on
a celebrity roller-coaster; the wife is on a toboggan with toddlers.

I read where Shari Theismann, at the time she
broke up with Joe, said, "If there is any single rule
for football wives, it's Don't Rock the Boat, especially during the season."

Baseball is no different. One of Mike's closest
friends in ball—right through two teams in the
majors—was running around. Mike knew it;
other teammates knew it. His wife was practically the last to know.

That's the thing about guys. They protect each
other. Something about all-for-the-team spirit.
Personally, I think it goes deeper. Guys, especially jocks, have this idea of scoring. It goes with
the game. You'll hear managers and coaches and
scouts talking about how "ribbies" separate the
big hitters from the banjos. (Ribbies is short for
R.B.I.'s, runs batted in.) In ball and out, the guys
don't want to louse up a teammate's scoring
capacity.

Gals just don't think that way. I don't know
too many who would protect one of their wives'
group who they knew was scoring.

If the guy is not making it—professionally, I mean—there is a whole other set of problems, and the wife is in the middle. I don't agree with Commissioner Peter Ueberroth in everything he's doing, but he's right that major league baseball should pay the cost of education for kids drafted into baseball directly out of high school who want to attend college. "The truth is, of those 300 or 400 players [minor leaguers], how many will make it to the major leagues? Forty? I don't feel very good about that. We have them in the minor leagues earning pennies for about four, five, six or seven years. They're married, have a couple of kids. They have no career, nowhere to start. They just kind of drop out of our system."

Mr. Ueberroth could be talking about kids on the teams we're managing. I've already mentioned Tony and Chris Ghelfi. Tony finished real strong with us at Kinston, but we were still concerned about his arm after two bouts of surgery on his pitching shoulder. In the following season of 1988 he not only did well at the AA level but was promoted midseason to the AAA club. Coaches and scouts talk about technical things that can't be corrected. There's no way a hitter who takes a big stride into a roundhouse swing is going to get by. Big league pitchers will have him talking to himself.

I've talked to enough scouts by now to know what their reports will show. With a "position" player—all but pitchers and catchers, that is—speed, bat power, and throwing strength are the major criteria. The first and third are God-given, unlikely to improve with experience. But there are whole books about hitting—Ted Williams,

Charley Lau, Pete Rose—and you hear all the time that Joe Doakes learned to hit only after he'd come under some expert's wing.

There are a few places on big league rosters for exceptions to the rules: players who have below-average speed, bat, and arm. We had one such at Kinston. This young infielder has something else God provided, though: quickness. And he's what watchers in this game call "coachable." He'll be playing in double and, hopefully, triple A for some years in hopes Cleveland or some other team might keep him on in a utility role.

It's a lot to ask of a wife to go five to seven years for, like Ueberroth said, pennies and then find not only no pot at the end of the rainbow but no rainbow, either.

Not every woman is cut out for it. Fans think it's all fun and games and glamour. Blame those flashes on your TV screen where we're dressed to the nines reading our cue cards to clap and look beautiful. Sure, we spend our husbands' bucks dolling up that way, but we also have to live with guys whose adolescence is being stretched. You read about extreme cases like Jim Bouton's, where he just couldn't cut it in the real world and keeps trying for comebacks in the boonies, trying to throw a knuckleball when his arm is dead.

NBC sports columnist Robert Lipsyte wrote an article about the tendency of football to prolong adolescence: "Indeed, so much of their swagger *is* adolescent; they walk and drive aggressively, they need to choose the television channel, win the video game, act as though they are in control while they are really totally dependent on other people—owners, coaches, agents, doctors, trainers. Those who 'rebel' are usually acting out some adolescent behavior—eccentric clothes, raucous conduct, drug abuse—that emphasizes their need to be directed" ("The Athlete's Losing Game," *New York Times Magazine* (Nov. 30, 1986), pp. 58–64).

And their need—o.k., I'll say it—to be pampered. You would expect their egos to be tremendous, but I have observed more often than not, it's the very opposite. Their ego is only as big or as little as the success or failure they had in their last game or season.

It is hard for these guys to grow up because everything is done for them. On road trips they have a schedule that tells them when to arrive at the airport—what airline, gate, and time. They are—literally—handed their boarding passes. They don't see their luggage again until they are at the hotel and it is brought up to their rooms. When they land at the airport, a charter bus awaits them. At the hotel, there is no waiting to check in; keys in envelopes with their names await them. The schedule tells them what time the bus will take them to the ballpark and what time it will return them to the hotel.

I notice how hard it is for Mike to take care of details when we travel in the off-season. Even though he's traveled mega-miles by plane, he gets impatient waiting for luggage. I'll often remind him I usually do it alone with four kids, one of whom is usually taking a ride on the luggage carousel.

Robert Lipsyte is right about the player carrying his competitiveness around with him off the field. Mike *needs* to beat his own kids in Candyland. He can't really enjoy a game of Horse in

163

our driveway without trying hard to win. He has to do the best he can in order to feel "comfortable." They are so used to being in control of everything on the field.

The one thing beyond control, of course, is the toll of the years. When you work as hard as they to remain in the shape necessary to perform, it is difficult to accept that their bodies can fail them at any time. There's just so much mileage in a pitcher's arm or quickness in a swing or resiliency in a fielder's reflexes.

The whole scene is unreal—although its end is too real—but the withdrawal is almost more than any of us can handle, for the player and the wife. Some players never give much thought to a life without ball. You can't really prepare for afterwards anyway. You owe it to yourself and your team not to worry about what you will do when ball is over.

I have seen players who take away from their effectiveness on the field planning for their future. They'll start a business on the side that will take too much of their time and too much from their game. We've been lucky from Mike's second season on to have put our finances in the capable hands of knowledgeable people. Some players get as involved in their investments as George Steinbrenner does with his team.

Life in the Big Show can't be matched anywhere, but it ends. Mike does not display his feelings easily, but I know he misses it all, including the very minuses he complained about during our twelve years up there: the clubhouse bickering, the pregame batting and fielding rituals, the same questions from the media season after season, an early afternoon game after a night game, having to rush for the airport to play the next night in another city. It has been tough for Mike to have had a part of his life taken away cold turkey.

The guys spend a lot of time together, play lots of pranks, share. When it ends, it ends (Yogi Berra again). All of a sudden you are on your own—no teammates—and you must start all over, in a hometown where you've lost touch. It was all there for the asking while you were playing. Now it's a new direction without direction—scary.

Some of the couples we have known take that new direction separately. We are doing it together

Designated Wives

W H E N after the 1986 New York–Penn season I knew I was serious about writing a wives' book on baseball, I wanted to bring in some of the gals I've known and tell something about their experiences. I made up a two-page questionnaire, which I mailed to the twenty women—all at some time wives in baseball—I felt I knew best. I asked them about their children; their trades and other moves, personal aspects; relationships with other wives; tips on moving, travel, maintaining morale; advantages/disadvantages of ball; worst situations faced; the good parts of being married to a ballplayer; best advice received and worst; best anecdote; life after retirement.

Of the 20, 12 responded—a high percentage, I am told. Now 12 out of an estimated 480 wives in the major leagues is a small sample. However, my dozen diamond darlings did much more than check off answers. They all wrote in detail—one a twenty-five-page letter, the others adding many pages to the questionnaire.

The letters are informal. There was no thematic order; they responded in the order of the questions. I have tried to keep to a narrative style so my girlfriends' ideas won't sound like replies to a survey.

Here are the names, with husbands' in parentheses:

Vickie (Alan) Bannister, Gloria (Buddy) Bell, Kristi (Doug) DeCinces, Peggy (Rich) Donnelly, Jan (Toby) Harrah, Jennifer (Ron) Hassey, Patti (Steve) Lake, Diane (Jeff) Newman, Cindy (Karl) Pagel, Janet (Jim) Sundberg, Patti (Don) Sutton, Annie (Rick) Waits.

Three phrases, either used or implied, kept turning up in the letters. "That's baseball!" "Nothing is forever!" "Travel light!" While it's possible that I am attracted to other wives who endorse my positive sentiments about baseball—and that those who voted yes to the game are attracted to me—I believe that even this small sampling reveals an in-favor consensus. From the minors on, we know that our husbands are fortunate to be among the 624 players in whom the right skills, fewest flaws, and luck combined to elevate them into the Big Show. For as little as one season plus (Cindy and Karl Pagel) and as many as twenty-three (Patti and Don Sutton), and with the exception of Peggy and Rich Donnelly, whose experience has been from the managing/coaching side, the couples are among baseball's crème de la crème, and none would have wished to miss the experience.

If you've been with me up to here, you'll understand why I consider trades, especially during the season, the endangering of our species. Susan (Mrs. Rick) Wise was even more direct in her letter responding to a note I placed in the *New York Times Book Review* about the book I was writing. Buying a house, she wrote, is "baseball's kiss of death." Now retired from ball, she and Rick twice bought houses in cities where they were playing and both times were traded before the following season. But Susan says the Wises have to take a back seat to their friends, Joe and Darlene Horner—Joe was a relief pitcher with many teams—who were on their way to the title company to close on their new house when on their car radio they heard that Joe had been traded.

Mike tells me that Rick Wise is a natural for a baseball nut's trivia question: For whom was Steve Carlton traded, one-for-one, from the St. Louis Cardinals to the Philadelphia Phillies in 1972? Steve went on to win 237 games in thirteen seasons with Philadelphia. Rick had made the all-star team both years before the trades, a factor in making Susan and him confident they wouldn't be traded and should buy houses.

Not all of us are like Susan and me—wives who like to own the house we come home to. When I tell you about Jennifer Hassey, you'll understand why the Hasseys have never bought during the season. In eleven years in the majors they lived in places that ranged from being free of rent —one hotel room, briefly—to rental places up to $2,600 a month. For two seasons—1985 and 1986—Ron was on a trade shuttle between the New York Yankees and the Chicago White Sox. I don't know of anything quite like what happened to Jennifer and Ron those two years.

The Chicago Cubs traded Ron to the Yankees for the 1985 season, and it was their best year ever. The Yankees do everything first-class for their players. The Yankee wives were one of the best groups Jennifer had known. Then the shuttle began. George Steinbrenner began it by trading Ron to the White Sox at the end of 1985. Three months later— in February, 1986—the White Sox traded Ron back to the Yankees. Then, after the All-Star-Game (on July 29, midseason), they were shocked when the Yankees traded him back to the White Sox. Ron learned of the latest trade after a night game; Jennifer learned about it while watching the game on TV.

The next night she watched her husband play on TV in a Chicago uniform. The day after that, an off-day, Ron returned to New York to pick up his things from his locker, kiss his kids goodbye, and leave Jennifer hasty (and familiar) instructions about (a) breaking the lease, (b) getting the rental furniture returned, and (c) deciding which day would work out best for them to fly into Chicago to find temporary accommodations—in a hotel, as it turned out—before returning to their permanent home in Tucson so the kids could get ready for school.

Not many of the wives I've come to know well could handle a scenario like that. From the time we first met Jennifer and Ron—that was in 1979, Mike's first year with the Indians—I never once saw Jennifer flustered. She has a way of simplifying tough situations. She helped me cope. When Ron was traded with Rick Sutcliffe to the Chicago Cubs after the 1984 season, it was like I had lost a solid friend. That was about the time everything began to sour for us in Cleveland, the year I could not afford to lose a Jennifer Hassey.

Not all trade stories are of the horror kind. The funniest I have ever heard comes from Vickie Bannister, who was with us 1980–83 in Cleveland. To get the full flavor of what happened to Vickie you have to know that she knew even less about ball in 1980, when she and Alan were married, than I knew at Great Bend and Liberal. Alan, who played all infield and outfield positions, was in his fifth year with the White Sox. Vickie, an R.N., went to work in a big Chicago hospital less than two weeks after the wedding. She had never seen a game, knew nothing about how or what Alan was paid. She knew nothing about trades and probably thought a relief pitcher was a container of cold water on a hot day. She had worked in medicine for a decade, but nothing enabled her to "doctor" the bills Alan was turning over to her for the start of the season. She had had little experience in flying but figured that with all the air travel they were doing in just those two weeks in April she had better go to work. Little did she know that, with a big leaguer's salary, anything she received would go to the IRS.

Vickie took a job on a coronary care floor where most of the patients were monitored. The news traveled fast that she was Alan Bannister's wife; soon people were asking her not only to provide Alan's autograph but her own. She had never worked in a major league–city hospital and had no idea how important baseball was to Chicagoans and how popular her husband was. She soon found out all about those things — and something else she didn't bargain for, what a trade means.

One night two months into the season she was sitting at the nurses' station charting when the monitor attached to the heart of a Mr. O'Connally went crazy. She jumped up and ran to his room. There was Mr. O'Connally, calling her name in a raving manner: "Vickie, Vickie, they've traded Alan! I can't believe it. Idiot White Sox, always trading off our good players!"

Alarms were going off everywhere. Other people were piling into the room. There Vickie sat, looking on in disbelief at the TV while Mr. O'Connally, who was not supposed to be out of bed, paced back and forth, ranting and completely unhooked from his monitor. "God, Vickie, they've traded Alan Bannister!"

It was not the end of the world; it was more — a baseball trade. Vickie had learned how unreal baseball is and how that unreal world can change after a trade. Why had the White Sox given Alan to someone else? Was he no good any more? Did they not like him? Why did Alan, who was happy in Chicago, let them send him to Cleveland?

Vickie, too, would learn to shrug and say, "That's baseball!"

Mike once said that Toby Harrah could fall into a bucket of shit and come out smelling like a rose. Jan Harrah answered my questionnaire after the 1986 season, Toby's last "guaranteed" season with the Rangers. At that time they were hoping for a coaching job in the Texas organization, but all he knew was that he would be going to Instructional League ("Sound familar?" she asked). Within a few weeks of her letter, we read that Toby had been named manager of the Rangers' triple-A team in Oklahoma City. At thirty-eight, he had skipped the usual stops at single A and double A—an unusual break, but not for Toby.

Jan wrote that Toby has always been at the right place at the right time, has rarely been injured, has always made a good salary, and has enjoyed the security of long-term contracts. He was the last player from the old Washington Senators to retire, having been a rookie on the 1971 Senators just before the team moved to Texas. He had played seven years with the Rangers, five with Cleveland, one with the Yankees, and the last two with the organization with which he started. Only the 1984 season under George Steinbrenner —first time he hadn't been a regular—was unhappy.

Mike and Toby, as players, never smelled the roses: the World Series. (I'm sure the possibility of managing a championship team is uppermost among their reasons for staying in the game.) Another of our earliest friends in ball— Jim Sundberg—did make it as first-string catcher for the world champion Kansas City Royals in 1985.

Janet Sundberg called the Series baseball's "top attraction" —to a wife, unlike any other experience. She and Jim joined Kansas City on a series of downers. They had been traded after a decade with the Rangers—the "Jim Sundberg Show" was a radio staple in the Dallas–Fort Worth area most of those years—and traded again after one mediocre year with Milwaukee. Janet, more than anyone I know, had made most of her friends outside baseball and she was initially unhappy in Kansas City. But when the Royals became the "miracle" team in 1985, down 0–2 to Toronto in the American League playoffs and winning; down 1–3 to St. Louis in the World Series—and winning in seven games—everything brightened.

Janet goes deep. She made an observation about how thankful she and Jim were that the World Series happened late in his career. If it had happened at the start, as it did with many of his teammates, they might have thought that

that was the way a whole career would go. It would be that much tougher to handle the game's pits. As it happened, after playing so long with teams that never made it, they weren't carried off in the clouds.

I thought of Janet's comment in connection with Bret Saberhagen, who had it all, including the Cy Young Award and World Series fame, at nineteen; but, at twenty, a losing record, injuries, despair.

Every baseball wife comes to realize that ball is a business, not a game. Some of us can even tick off the exact date. I said in the previous chapter that for me it was June 14, 1979, when we were traded from San Diego to Cleveland. That it turned out to be career saving for Mike doesn't change the message I got then and still get now. Ball players are just so many pieces of meat, as Kristi DeCinces charged in her letter. We met Kristi and Doug during the trip to Japan in 1976. Although they never played together, Doug and Mike have kept in touch ever since. Kristi is unassuming, so we made a good pair. She writes just about the best letters of any of my girlfriends in baseball. Naturally, I was expecting more than a routine letter. She didn't let me down.

Doug was on Gene Mauch's California Angels team that came within one out of beating Boston and getting into the World Series in 1986. Kristi recalled the unburied-dead atmosphere on the Los Angeles–to-Boston charter after Doug's team had lost the fifth game after leading most of the way. She's such a fine writer, I just have to quote her:

> If I had been a manager, an owner, a G.M., I would have been parading up and down the aisle lifting up the spirits of those stunned, defeated human beings in hopes of bestowing on them that extra confidence they always need no matter how "together" they may seem to the public (and even to each other). Maybe they still would have gone on to lose, but the power

management has over these players is all too rarely a positive one. We all hear the negatives about players, especially during contract negotiations, but how often does management express faith and confidence in a player who is in a valley of his career? Could it make a difference if management knew their power and channeled it more productively?

The power of management is even more overwhelming when a player is marginal; when it is touch-and-go between staying in the Big Show as a part-time player or going back to riding buses. Cindy Pagel wanted only two things in life: (1) to see Karl make it in the majors; and (2) to raise a family.

The Pagels' eight years were mostly in the minor leagues. In 1980, after world-class stats at Wichita in triple A, Karl became one of those players "to be named later" by the Cubs in a trade with Cleveland for Cliff Johnson. If the trade had meant the Pagels were going to Cleveland, they would have been revved up, but all it meant was that they had to uproot at Wichita and set themselves down in yet another triple-A city.

Cindy can't understand how Karl, who was primed for the Cubs both as an outfielder and first baseman and who had been so sensational for their triple-A farm team, was reduced to throw-in status.

Karl was playing golf when the call came. Cindy's sister and brother-in-law were houseguests. It was the last time they would ever know a comfortable routine. That was 1980. The 1982 season, even though ten weeks of it was with the Indians, where we got to know Cindy and Karl, was even more agonizing. They began at Charleston, got called up by Cleveland in June, had only eighteen at-bats in those six weeks. They were hanging by a thread the whole time. Sure enough, in August, with just two weeks left of the triple-A season, they were shuttled back to Charleston.

Because they played mainly in the minors for eight seasons, Karl never made any big money. In 1982, with all the shuffling around, they had a tax bill of $1,100. Karl was in spring training, once again a hair's breadth (always the way) from being sent down. He could or would only think about his chances on the field. It was left up to her whether to get a loan.

Cindy's big point is that financial problems and decisions should be shared by husband and wife. She has no doubt that they never got a fair shake in ball. Who knows why or, even more sad, does anyone care? Cindy knows the nebulous *they*—that is, whoever called the shots—wrecked Karl's career. They barely got a whiff of the "good life." She knows there's luck involved—being in the right place at the right time, like Toby Harrah—but there's more politics in baseball than outsiders know.

Cindy is not bitter about some other player who held down Karl's position. I know because that player was my husband. Neither is Kristi DeCinces, although Doug waited four years as heir apparent to Brooks Robinson's third-base job on the Orioles. Cindy Pagel always thought that if the Cubs or Indians—*they*—had really wanted Karl, they would have found a spot for him. She could never understand how wives would so often talk about hating so-and-so because that player was preventing their man from making the team.

How does the wife of a player who had been with one organization for sixteen years accept the pink ticket? Peggy Donnelly was disappointed—but mostly hurt—not only at the news but at the way it was handled. With Rich, it was the Rangers, but his story can be duplicated a thousand times with every team in ball.

Peggy, who as I've said was my first role model, has never been able to understand the disregard for the personal side of a player's life. After Rich got into management she learned two things: (1) baseball is a business; and (2) the only time it ever humanizes is when a rare owner forgets the player is meat and remembers he has a family.

G.M.'s, farm directors, field managers, and coaches are Company people. They receive business directives. Most carry them out to the letter. Then there is that unique group that remember human beings live inside the uniform.

Diane Newman received the phone call while on vacation in Maui. It was five days before Christmas 1982. Jeff and Tony Armas had been traded by Oakland to Boston for Carney Lansford and Gary Hancock. They were devastated. They had been with Oakland for seven good years, and Jeff had three years left on his five-year contract.

They had just added on to their house ("the curse") and felt, like Mike and I did at Texas, that they were going to be in Oakland for the rest of his playing days. Jeff, a catcher, even had a two-year addition to his contract to work for the A's after his playing days.

Diane and Jeff felt like their family had turned them out, banishing them to the East Coast, to an unfamiliar part of the world. Their oldest was in junior high and couldn't leave school for the first two and a half months of the 1983 season. He had ball games of his own. Now they were going to be separated for more than just road trips. It was the toughest adjustment of their lives.

Although my questionnaire didn't ask directly how the wives thought their husbands would handle the inevitable comedown from the image sports provides, their answers showed they know all about the problem.

Janet Sundberg noted that there is a paradox about baseball—maybe all professional sports—involving the children and the player-husbands. Life in baseball has made the Sundberg kids more mature than most children their age. Yet baseball often seems intent on keeping the husbands—the kids' fathers—forever children. Part of the problem is that many teams treat their players like kids instead of having adult-to-adult relationships.

Peggy Donnelly knew, quite simply, that there could be no life for Rich outside of baseball. He planned to stay in coaching/managing forever. If they were out of pro ball, they would resurface on a field somewhere. Then there's always the fate, dreaded by many wives, of becoming a scout with that job's inevitable by-products: sudden calls, often without notice, to be in unlikely places and, for the most part, low pay. When the Rangers rejected him after sixteen years, Rich's world crumbled—until another coaching job opened. Now he's with Pittsburgh. For Rich, what's after sports? Peggy had to say it: Death.

Kristi DeCinces found that "this thing of being a celebrity" was both her and Doug's toughest nut to crack. They would often have rather blended in. To Kristi, her husband didn't appear to have any problem with the realization that the fifteen-year unreality was likely to end after the 1987 season. (It didn't—quite. Doug played in Japan with the Yakult Swallows in 1988, joining such ex-big leaguers as Tony Bernazard, Warren Cromartie, Mike Easler, Terry Harper, Matt Keough, Bill Madlock, and George Wright in the Orient.)

For Cindy Pagel the hardest thing she ever had to deal with was Karl's release from baseball. She knew, after the long years in the minors, that he no longer had the desire to play. He was ready to hang 'em up. It was hard for her not to pressure him. She loved the baseball life, but she loves Karl more.

Patti Sutton looks to the time, not long off, when she will have Don home at night. Going on twenty-three years in the majors as the 1988 season approached, Patti looked forward to going on summer vacations that have nothing to do with ball; to letting dad take part in all the kids' things, especially their school adventures.

Patti Lake, like Susan Wise, saw my newspaper ad and

replied. She noted that Steve is one of those kids signed right out of high school. Steve was thirty in 1987, not a young age for a catcher, and he had not a single credit toward a college degree and no other training than baseball. People on the outside don't realize how few ever make star salaries and how quickly moving expenses and/or rental payments or mortgages eat up savings.

When I watched Patti Lake's husband make a bruising put-out at home plate on the onrushing Gary Gaetti in the 1987 World Series, I thought of Patti's long letter of nine months earlier, which was almost 100 percent regretful. Now that she and Steve have "smelled the roses," would she tell a different story? Her answer is contained in the Appendix.

Alan and Vickie Bannister got out of baseball altogether after his declaration of free agency, like Mike's, did not bring any takers after the 1985 season. He was ready. Five years before his retirement Alan became interested in real estate investing. He began to educate himself and dabble in the market. By 1986, he had enough knowledge and experience that an investment advisory firm whose clients are exclusively baseball players offered him a position in their real estate division. "Now we are the average 9 to 5 suburban family in Mesa, Arizona," Vickie wrote. "The challenge of his new work is equal to what baseball provided. And, with all his clientele from familiar settings, Alan feels as if he's still close to the game." (It's worth noting here that, only two years out of the game, Alan finds himself back in the game as a Class-A manager in the Montreal organization.)

Once we wives accept the sometimes harsh terms of life in baseball, the trick is to lighten those terms, modify them, make them tolerable. Take the whole matter of travel. Many of these pages have been devoted to its logistics. Most of the letters discussed travel but with little more advice than Travel light!

Janet Sundberg writes that some of her best memories

date from the Rangers' minor-league camp—autumn, 1972 —when she, Jim, Mike, and I fought the battle of Plant City and its cockroaches and poor plumbing. "We were all in a state of 'blessed ignorance,'" she writes. "If I knew then what I know now I might have been worried." She remembers the way I packed. "You waited till the day we left to start, just throwing things in suitcases and off you went. No three days of panic like me." What Janet may not know is that more than fourteen years, four kids, and one large van later, that's pretty much still the way I pack.

Most of my girlfriends either did what I would have done with the "travel tips" on the questionnaire—pass—or, like Jennifer Hassey, simply said, "Try to fly as often as you can," or, like Patti Lake, "You fear packing all through the off-season but when spring comes everything becomes instinctive again."

Vickie Bannister and Peggy Donnelly refused to duck the problem. Vickie put it this way:

If I were to write a book for baseball wives, I would address it to moving and travelling. For now, though, I'll stick to one theme: travel light! I used to make a game out of seeing how little I could get by with. As I said before, I was inducted into marriage and baseball the same year. I couldn't wait to nest. Who wants to nest in a barn? It took me only that first season—two moves, each requiring Mayflower—to forget about linen tablecloths, china, and special pictures on the walls. By our final season I was down to beds, clothes, and a TV. Even with two babies under the age of two, we didn't even pack a highchair.

Peggy answered more specifically:

I'll answer this one by suggesting the best buys a/o wedding gifts for anyone contemplating a career as head of a baseball family. I'll limit myself to 6. (Remember, dear reader, Rich and I have been mostly coaching in the minors.)

1. A van or station wagon. (A semi is really best, but the players' parking lots in most minor-league parks never allow enough space.)

2. Toaster oven.

3. Electric skillet.

4. Large green garbage bags. Really. They will mash into any space; can be re-packed with a season's acquired junk. There are drawbacks (so never be without a suitcase or two). The bags don't go over real well in hotel lobbies or on airlines.

5. Thermos. Mostly so the kids can have soft drinks at the park without paying those ridiculous prices. I know families who give half their salary back to the owners at the nachos and coke stands.

6. A can opener.

If I didn't think I could paraphrase Vickie and Peggy on travel tips, how can I with these gals' remarks about their kids? Only one item in the questionnaire dealt directly with kid stuff. That didn't stop these mothers from writing lots about their broods. The ages of the wives' kids are as of the time I received the questionnaires, in 1986.

According to Janet Sundberg (Aaron, 14; Audra, 10; Briana, 3),

> It's not being alone that bothers me except it always seems like things go wrong when they are on the road. During my third pregnancy I went into premature labor. When my pediatrician tried to stop the labor, the baby went into fetal distress and did not survive delivery. I was just starting my eighth month. So close yet so far away.
>
> Of course Jim was as far away as he could possibly be and still be within the continental limits: Seattle.

When he learned that we had lost the baby—the day of
the last game in Seattle—he tried to check on a flight
to Texas but none would have left before the team
charter. So he stayed and got home at 1 A.M. It was the
worst thing I had ever been through and hard not to resent Jim and baseball for his not being there. This was
also the year of the baseball strike—1981. Three weeks
after I lost the baby the teams stopped playing. Jim
and I spent two months regrouping. It proved the best
summer of our career. I guess that's how bad we
needed the time together.

Gloria Bell (David, 14; Michael, 11½; Ricky, 7; Kristi, 4½;
Traci, 1), noted that

Dads miss a lot of important things—kids sports, their
graduations, holidays, and picnics. Right now, the successful heart surgery on Traci, our fifth child, combined with Buddy's trade from Texas to Cincinnati,
which is home for both of us, had made this year, although late in our career, one of the best. I agree with
you, Sharon, that taking the kids out of school, especially in their early years, has been more than compensated for by all they've seen and done in our travels. We used to take them to spring training every
year, but as the three boys get older I'm cutting down
on the length of time we go to Florida. I'm just glad
the boys have had the experience of baseball. If Buddy
should decide not to stay in the game, the two girls,
being so young, won't really miss it.

Kristi DeCinces (Timothy, 12; Amy, 10) described her son's
birth thus:

Timothy was born in Rochester, N.Y., in 1974, the year
Brooks Robinson was *supposed* to retire. Doug had the
best spring training of anyone on the team but at the
last minute was sent down to triple-A in Rochester be-

cause Brooks had decided not to retire and the Orioles wanted Doug to play every day. (This was so painful at the time but turned out to be best for Doug in the long run.) Not only did poor Doug have this pain to deal with, but he was about to become a father for the first time two weeks after he was sent down.

We had nothing lined up in Rochester as we had been led to believe this was to be his year to make the big-league team, but—surprise—off we went to Upstate New York to get the *very* pregnant, *very* hysterical mother-to-be settled in. I couldn't wait for Doug to complete his time in the minor-league camp or I would have been too close to my due date. So up we flew to find an apartment to rent and furniture to rent and a doctor for me. Then back to Florida to finish camp, only to return, by the grace of God, to witness our son's birth on *opening day* (no less!).

Jennifer Hassey (Brad, 7; Kimberly, 5½; Dana, 2½) remembered living arrangements:

I laugh the hardest when I remember one of the worst living arrangements we had to endure. We were living in Chicago, in that gorgeous high-rise condominium (forty-third floor) I've already mentioned—with three small children (five, four, three months). Dana was in her port-a-crib in a closet off the master bedroom. We had so much laundry I used to put it in extra-large garbage bags and throw it on the double stroller and roll it downstairs to the laundromat. The kids learned "elevator etiquette," always letting ladies with strollers out first. They knew exactly how to enter and exit a taxi as well as hold on for dear life. Brad found his own private backstop by throwing the nerf ball against the living room wall. Poor Dana became so fat because she had a bottle in her mouth all night long so that the neighbors wouldn't hear her fuss and cry in the middle of the night.

Vickie Bannister (Lacey, 3; Ashley, 2) linked her most memorable times to her children:

Pretty much all my most memorable experiences — both good and bad — revolve around Lacey and Ashley. Lacey is our adopted child. She caught us by surprise by arriving a month premature. I was in Florida visiting my family; Alan, playing with the Indians, was in Milwaukee on a road trip. We were living in Cleveland for the season; Lacey was born in California; and we were adopting through the State of Arizona, our legal residence. By the time we were tracked down and I could get to the West Coast via standby and three transfer flights the baby was 14 hours old. Thank God for our Moms. I was really out of it with excitement; Mom went along for moral support and pulled everything together. By the time I got to the hospital it was 3 A.M. I was so nervous that I couldn't get my identification out of my wallet. They gave me a rocking-chair and brought the baby to me. I just sat there, holding her and rocking until the sun began to come up.

Alan and I had talked to each other by phone at least a dozen times by then and he was trying to think of a name for her. He had found a baby name book somewhere and each time I talked to him he had suggestions from further down the alphabet. By dawn he was down to the L's. "This one I love," he said. "Lacey."

It fit her perfectly — so tiny and feminine. I told Alan and he began to cry. There he was alone in a hotel in Milwaukee. He wanted to see Lacey so bad that he had decided to fly out against the wishes of the manager, Jeff Torborg. Fortunately, I was able to get Alan's dad to talk him out of leaving the team. His dad promised he would see that we got back to Cleveland as soon as possible.

The next few days were filled with getting interstate transit papers so we could take Lacey out of state. Our social worker in Arizona said he would have to see her in my possession; I would have to sign papers. We arranged a layover in Phoenix where the caseworker would meet us at the airport to complete the paperwork. Three days later she was released from the hospital and we headed straight for the Los Angeles airport. I was so happy to be heading for home in Arizona. However, we were stopped; I would not be permitted to fly with so young a baby.

My knees about collapsed but not so much that I didn't talk to everyone who was anyone with the airline, finally convincing them of my urgency. They had me sign 49 releases and an hour later we were on a plane to Phoenix. The delay in California shortened our time in Phoenix. Would the caseworker be there? Even if he were, would there be enough time to make our connection to Cleveland?

He was. We did. We pushed the luggage cart fitfully while I signed complicated papers that I was unable to read. By the time Lacey was a year old she had been on 12 airlines flights, lived in five cities, and had a little sister.

Annie Waits (Kathryn Elizabeth, 6; Michael McGinness, 3; John Bradley, 6 months) bemoaned her nomadic lifestyle:

I would be so glad for a "boring" lifestyle; to be a homebody, never having to move again (I'd like to live and die in the house we're in right now.). Rick shares my distaste for single parenting, the kids often having no father. He misses out on the everyday communication that makes my children and me so close. My kids actually prefer me, when asked to make a choice, and this must sadden their dad, although we both realize the favoritism is due to my proximity.

183

I feel it is preferable for a child to begin school with classmates than to have to come in late when cliques are formed and classroom behavior and expectations are established. So I come home early to put Kathryn in school at the beginning of the school year, but I take her out early in the summer. We are fortunate that spring training is only up the road in Phoenix. Sometimes I am resentful that I am not home to do summer camp with fellow schoolmates.

Diane Newman (Tom, 16; Ryan, 6) described school problems:

You realize our 16-year-old was Jeff's son by a previous marriage (just joking). Except for first grade, school wasn't a real problem, for Jeff's first 7 years were in the same place—with the A's. We would take Tom out for spring and either put him in school or get a tutor in Arizona. It worked out great. Tom is very outgoing and jumped right in with the new kids. When Jeff was traded to Boston, we realized we couldn't move as easily so we stayed home while Dad lived alone for 2½ months in Boston. Once school was out, we moved to Boston for the summer. We all missed our daddy and he us, too.

And Patti Lake (Ryan, 5; Brendan, 2; Jordan, 4 mos.) remarked on Dad's split identity.

The kids are too young to appreciate their dad's status. They believe everyone's dad is on TV. Going to the ballpark is strictly for social reasons. The boys refer to their dad as "Steve Lake" when he's in uniform.

It's a commonplace to say that there would be no baseball without fans. Anyone who goes to a lot of games knows that fans divide into bystanders—onlookers, if you will—and the boo-birds. Not all the wives in my survey have adjusted to the latter. It'is not easy when the object of those boos is your husband. Some fans insist it's their right to say just about anything for the price of admission. In a way, I have to agree. That is one of the interesting things about sports: they allow an outlet for many people to scream, yell, cuss out loud. I have always thought that most fans do not mean what they say personally when they are screaming ugly things about your husband. I doubt if many of them would say bad things about your husband if they knew they were sitting next to his wife and family.

My way of dealing with someone within my hearing saying bad things about Mike was finding a friend—usually another baseball wife—and asking them to stop by later to make sure the dude who was doing all the bad-mouthing knew who I was.

The saddest part is watching the foul comments hurting your kids. That's their daddy who is taking the heat. It breaks my heart. One time I remember a fan really being on Mike's case in Cleveland and Kim just looking back at the guy, turning around, staring at Mike on first base, and just letting the tears come.

The NBC cameraman who played his lens on Patty Blyleven during the 1987 American League Championship Series in Minnesota and Detroit knew what he was doing. For one thing, Patty is photogenic; for another, she says (and acts) what she thinks. There was this one night in Cleveland. I could never have done it, but it was wonderful. Bert Blyleven was pitching poorly. Some fan close to the family section was just giving him fits. Patty just turned around and told the jerk to shut up or get out. He came right back and said he had paid his $8 and could say whatever he wished. Patty took out her billfold, wrote out a check for eight bucks, gave it to the guy, and requested he go elsewhere and try something else that would be more enjoyable.

My Grandma Gee Gee usually knows what she is doing.

One time she did a lot of good for a young fiancée without knowing. Jeff Burroughs made American League Most Valuable Player in 1974, the same year Mike was Rookie of the Year. The 1975 season was nothing but a struggle for Jeff. The fans were really getting to him. This one night Jeff's fiancée, Debbie, now his wife, was sitting next to Gee Gee, but Gee Gee had no idea who she was. While the fans nearby were giving Jeff a hard time, Debbie leaned over and asked my grandmother what she thought of Jeff. "Well, he's having a rough time," answered Gee Gee in typical well-thought-out words, "but he is an excellent player. What do you think of him?" Debbie said she thought he was pretty neat, especially since he would soon be her husband.

Most stadiums have wives' sections or family sections. They offer some protection from the boo-birds. In San Diego, where so much else was wrong, we had the first four rows of boxes in one concentrated area. This was good because you knew if someone was sitting in those first four rows they were family. You learned not to let the people you brought say anything about the players.

I was never one to let the kids get out of eyeshot in those big stadiums. You don't have to be an alarmist to know that the youngster of one of the new millionaires in baseball might be at risk. In Cleveland we had to have a policeman sometimes take us across the street. At night some ball-yards are scary.

Sal Bando's wife, Sandy, was assaulted in the Milwaukee parking lot. She was seven months pregnant. A guy attacked her just as she was about to get in her car. In summer, 1987, a guy followed Diane Caudill from the hotel in Oakland to the parking lot. Fortunately, Bill was nearby to rescue her. He broke his hand in the process and missed the final month.

Some of the teams are at last providing better protection for us.

Our final questions came down to the best and worst about their careers as wives in big league baseball. Here, alphabetically and perhaps a bit boiled down, are the replies.

Vickie Bannister:
Best: The pride I have in Alan for having worked so hard to become one of the select few.
Worst: Alan's twice being unable to be with me at the time our two babies arrived. First, as noted, not being able to accompany me to pick up our adopted child; second, not being able to be with me for the birth of our natural child. I don't feel so bad for myself as I do for Alan. The experiences became mine. He was the one who had to sacrifice.

Gloria Bell:
Best: Not having financial problems; getting to the ball-games—so much fun, the boys have loved it; spring training was always our treat.
Worst: Being alone at first, then having so many responsibilities alone.

Kristi DeCinces:
Best: Probably the opportunities of many kinds—travel, financial comfort, and being able to help others in both a financial and emotional way.
Worst: Probably being a "celebrity" when at times just wanting to blend in.

Peggy Donnelly:
Best: Most of the time you're "special." People smile at you more, open doors, give you free tickets and great seats. When it's good it's really good: people tell you you're wonderful, you're written up, there are always gifts, on and on.
Worst: When it's bad it's horrid. If he makes an error

187

or goes o-for-20, that's when help is needed but is hard to find.

Jan Harrah:
Best: The never-a-dull moment lifestyle; the excitement in the game both Toby and I love; the financial security.
Worst: The constant relocating; saying goodbye to dear friends.

Jennifer Hassey:
Best: People are immediately friendly; easy to strike up conversations.
Worst: The other side of the above: the tendency to question the validity of friendships; Ron's injury.

Patti Lake:
Best: Seeing my kids' names in the paper when they were born.
Worst: Seeing the pain Steve has gone through for baseball, physically and mentally, and how it's rewarded him.

Diane Newman:
Best: The life, the travel; seeing people and places we might never have been able to.
Worst: Road trips; watching my husband sitting and waiting rather than taking charge of a situation.

Cindy Pagel:
Best: Being able to spend lots of quality time with my husband; avoidance of the routine by the sheer uncertainty of things; life a constant learning experience.
Worst: Karl's release from baseball.

Janet Sundberg:
Best: The World Series; the "counselling" training; knowing I'm a viable part of his career.

Worst: Conditional love; management's less than attractive view of wives.

Patti Sutton
Best: Seeing Don win his 300th game in June of '86; the hum of excitement as Don came closer; seeing Don's teammates surround him; Don's face; the children's too.
Worst: Over all, the road trips. As a pitcher's wife, I am more tense in his 23rd season than I was 20 years ago. I can't explain it.

Annie Waits:
Best: Very few ever realize their childhood dream. My husband is in that very small minority. It is nice to be married to someone who loves what he is doing.
Worst: Baseball had made our lives hectic, has taken my husband away so much of the time, and has prevented him from knowing his children; the frustration of a 2–13 season, watching Rick ache and hurt — listening to a losing game on radio — and not being there to help and unable to do so even if I was there.

Major in the Minors

I T doesn't seem by mere chance that we landed in Williamsport, Pennsylvania, for Mike's third season in the dugout. Williamsport is the home of Little League, and it was last summer that Andy, at six, was old enough to begin playing.

Ever since Mike left to manage Instructional the first time, Andy has had a hard time letting me out of his sight. I believe it is because he has watched his dad pull out of the driveway for many a road trip. Nothing unusual in that except he kept not coming home. Andy probably began thinking the same disappearing act might happen with his mom.

We began calling him Velcro instead of Tank (we literally stuck together).

Velcro was not overly enthusiastic when I took him to the Original Little League park for first practice. As I might have predicted, Mike couldn't be there. Maybe that was for the best, for it took a lot of patience for me to get Andy to let go of me and start playing—about an hour and fifteen minutes' worth. I knew if he could get past his being-shy stage, he would love playing.

Later, when I was describing Andy's shyness to Mike and one of his pitchers, my husband said it was lucky for Andy

Here are Tom Chandler, the manager,
and Mike with Andy, 4½, getting ready
for a game at Batavia in the New York–Penn
League, summer, 1986.

that I had chaperoned the deal, as Mike would have busted
Andy's butt within five minutes and that would have been
the beginning and the end of Andy's career in ball. The
pitcher chimed in with an extenuating circumstance that
neither Mike nor I had considered. What must it have
looked like to Andy, after three years in the minor leagues,
watching kids his own age or a year older who could barely
throw, let alone catch, a ball? "It's tough to go from playing AA to T-ball," the pitcher said. He was referring to
Andy's heading out to the park early with Mike and tossing the ball with real players at every home game.

His comment also strikes to the heart of a major advantage of returning to the minors. Our kids—but especially
Andy—are more involved in what Dad does. Andy puts on

his official Indians' uniform even on those days the Williamsport Bills are on the road. All the players serve their term and play with him. About a month into the season Andy started pestering Mike to let him sit close to the dugout during the games. Mike reluctantly agreed to let him sit with Jeff Sampsell, who videotapes our hitters. Mike's ground rules to Andy were explicit:

Mike: Now Andy, you know you can't be talking to me during the game.

Andy: Yes Dad, I won't.

Mike: If you need anything you must go to Mom and ask her. If you need to go to the restroom, if you need money for the concessions, or anything else, go to your Mom.

Andy: O.K. Dad.

Mike: If you ever want to sit here again, and I want you to, then you must remember that Daddy is doing his job and must concentrate on the game and can't be talking to you. O.K.?

Andy: O.K. Dad, *O.K.* I promise.

Not that Andy is not a man of his word and not that he didn't really try. He did just fine while the bad guys were batting top of the first inning. But when it came our turn to bat, a fair promise began to fade.

Andy: Dad.

(*Mike:* He's just forgotten. I'll just ignore him and he'll remember.)

Andy: Dad! (A little louder.)

Mike turns and looks straight at Andy, giving him his best raised-eyebrow look but without a word. He returns his gaze to the field.

Andy: Dad, you don't have a first-*baserman* coach!

Mike glances toward the first base coaching box, which does seem to be vacant. "Somebody get out there and coach first."

It's funny how we see one another pretty exclusively in the role that touches us. To me, Mike is my husband; to the kids, he is their dad; to the players, he is the manager. One of our players, pitcher Paul Kuzniar, has caused Mike some real headaches—and he's a Texas boy too. P. K., as he's called, once got the message how Mike felt about him when he asked what he would do to him if he were his son.

"P. K., if you were my son, all that would be left of you would be a couple of strands of hair on that wall. I would hang you from the wall."

The next time Mike lost it with P. K. you could tell by the shocked look on the kid's face when he came out of the locker room. P. K. came right over to where Kim and I were standing and began relating the story to us. He spoke mainly to Kim, who had just entered her teens. "Has your Dad ever been so mad at you that his jaw juts out and his bottom lip begins to quiver?"

Kim, who was smiling from ear to ear, said "Yep."

"Does he make you look him in the eye when he's talking to you?"

"Yep."

"Well, I try but I just can't do it. Skip keeps yelling at me to look at him when he's talking to me. I did the best I could, but I was really looking just a hair above his eyes. I just couldn't look him right in the eyes."

If I know my husband, he was having a worse time than P. K. Maybe Mike would be better off if he could remain just one person to his players—their manager. But unlike any manager I have known outside Dave García, Mike can't be just the manager. He cares about these guys and wants nothing but the best for each. At times his caring gets in the way of his instructing, but you wouldn't want it any other way. They say Dick Williams, a very successful big-league manager, always intimidated his players. Too much a perfectionist, no room for the personal. I think Mike's way has the best chance.

I, too, cannot be just the manager's wife. Lucky for me, unlike some managers who prefer that their wives have

Manager Mike and his friend Steve Comer,
the pitching coach, watch a performance
by the Kinston, North Carolina, team
in the Carolina League.
Courtesy Cleveland Plain Dealer.

nothing to do with the players' wives, Mike encourages me
to be there for these girls. We have been in this game long
enough to know how crucial a wife's attitude can be to every
married guy on the field.

You can't have read this far without figuring me out as
wanting to be in the middle of everything. I sit with the
wives at all the home games. I am at the point where it
won't be long before I'll be old enough to be some of their
mothers. Actually, at thirteen, Kim is closer to their ages
—early twenties, most of them—than I am. I still think I
know what they are thinking and feeling.

One reason Mike is successful with these young guys
coming up is that they know he has been there. From Ba-

tavia to Williamsport, you can sense the respect. And I feel like the gals look to me, too, when the going gets tough. They know I've been there.

Believe me, the going does get tough. I wish we had a clear-cut winner of the Williamsport Wives Walking Wounded award for 1988. Some of my gals have been dragged from coast to coast for four or five years already. Some have endured moves within the season; some have had to survive injuries and surgery—sometimes several times. I've read where a bone surgeon will come right out and say the human knee was not constructed to withstand football. Sometimes I wonder if the human arm was ever constructed to toss a baseball ninety miles an hour. One of the acid tests for a baseball wife—a pitcher's wife—is how many operations on her man's arm, each one necessitating a new start, she can bear up under.

How many wives will put their own careers—often, too, the bearing of children—on indefinite hold against the long odds their guy will make it to the Show?

Maybe I'm biased a bit because like me she's a Texas gal, but I think I'll nominate Dana Hilton for that Wives Walking Wounded prize. She and Stan Hilton have been bobbing up and down in the minors for six years now. Stan starred for Baylor in the early 1980s, and the Oakland Athletics drafted him as their No. 1 pick in the June, 1983, draft. He injured his arm his rookie season and had to sit out all the next season after arm surgery. He stuck with the A's organization for a season and a half, but the A's didn't stick with him. After a couple of "lost" seasons, Stan and Dana joined Williamsport the last half of last season. When nothing happened between seasons, he remained on the Bills' roster for 1988.

But with significant differences. Mike, in consultation with the Cleveland brass, has converted Stan Hilton from starting pitcher to middle reliever. For a pitcher that means a whole different regimen. Instead of his accustomed psyching himself for action every fourth or fifth day, Stan has had to ready himself to come in from the bullpen at any time. I've got to resort to baseball words to explain Stan's new role with the Bills. Typically, he would come into a game in the middle innings, hold down the opposition while (Mike hoped) we would get a lead, and then give way to Kevin Wickander, our ace stopper, who almost always mopped up. For most of the season they were a good combination—Kevin at one point in midseason pitched 23⅓ consecutive scoreless innings.

I have already explained why pitchers, not being position players, live with special kinds of stress. But even more than the pitchers themselves, I have always felt particular empathy for their wives. They sure have to stay loose. Being one of us Texas females, Dana has had strict yet loving upbringing. She has needed both facets this season.

Like all of us, Dana set up housekeeping in Williamsport —not an easy task in a city where everyone insisted on one-year leases. While on a road trip the first month, Stan got the call to report to AAA. He phoned Dana that he would be leaving for Colorado Springs from Glens Falls in the morning. She would need to dispatch him a suit of clothes by UPS since AAA players travel by plane and are required to wear suits. She was not, however, to pack until Stan knew how permanent the move would be.

Dana took the uncertainty in her usual graceful style and hung loose for two weeks before getting the word from Cleveland to go ahead and move to Colorado. While three of us wives helped Dana with the packing, I kept referring to how Kathy Comer, pregnant and not well, had managed to join Steve in Cleveland last year at Kinston. This would be a piece of cake in comparison. I masterminded the loading of their Blazer, and Brian Allard, our pitching coach, changed the oil. Dana spent the night in our apartment and headed out for Pittsburgh next morning, where she was to be joined by Stan's dad.

We wives followed the next legs in Dana's journey by telephone. Two days later she pulled into home territory (Dallas), took care of some business, saw her folks briefly, thanked her father-in-law for his help with the driving, and headed for Colorado Springs alone. Twelve hours later the Hiltons were reunited at the Hilton.

The next day they signed their second lease of the season. Dana repeated a familiar ritual. She unpacked, got phone and cable hooked up and all utilities turned on, and settled in for the remaining three months of the season.

Until a major-league team has exhausted the number of times it can option a player to its minor-league affiliate, the unseasoned player may find himself on a not-so-merry shuttle. For him, time is measured not in hours and days but by the reinstatement of disabled players—established players, usually—to the active roster. When someone comes back on the roster, someone else must come off. Usually the expendable player(s) is (are) the most recent addition(s).

They are the Stan Hiltons.

Two days after their reunion in Colorado Springs, Stan went on yet another road trip with his new team, and Dana found herself alone again in an unfamiliar apartment. Although the new wives were there for her, Dana missed her counterparts in Williamsport. She had only the telephone for comfort, and after three days of the nail-biting loneliness every young baseball wife knows but can't accept, she dialed Chris Ghelfi's number. That night at the ballpark, a variation on the Hiltons' familiar story was played for us. None of us is likely to forget it.

Chris had just finished relating Dana's report on how much she missed us when someone from the ticket office came into the wives' section to tell me I had a phone call. Such calls are nearly always emergencies and, thank goodness, rare. Was Grandma Gee Gee sick? Some other trouble back in Perryton? When I answered with a weak hello, I heard a familiar voice. It was Dana. She was crying. "Guess

what? We're coming back to Williamsport." Stan had just
phoned her from the road to tell her they were being sent
back down to AA.

Six days. She had been out there only six days. It made
me sick. It was all I could do not to cry along with her.
I tried to be strong and look at the good side. "Well, at least
you'll be back here with all of us. . . . Maybe your apartment
hasn't been rented yet and you can just move back into it."
Nothing was any good. I felt better when we had both had
a good cry.

Long distance is the next best thing to being there. I've
never been able to take those Cliff Robertson commercials
for A.T.&T. lightly. By the time Dana had rung off, she knew
that while it wouldn't be easy she could move back where
we would all be there to get her resettled.

Luckily, Mike and Steve Swisher, the Colorado Springs
manager, saw Stan's situation humanely and—rare in this
game—looked beyond the teams' needs to Dana's and Stan's.
Stan was given permission to drive across country with his
wife. Had I trained Mike well or hadn't I?

Three hours later I phoned Dana to see if her spirits had
lifted in light of new developments. She was herself again.
Carla Medina, the wife of one of the Colorado Springs players, had also heard the news (I've mentioned how fast news
of promotions and demotions travels in baseball). They
already had Dana's apartment packed—again. Next day Stan
flew back to Colorado Springs and they made the twenty-
six-hour drive to meet our team—where? In Reading—on
the road again.

Dana spent two days with Stan in Reading—that made
eight days out of thirty—and the seven after that with me
while we looked for an apartment. By the time Stan and
the team came home, the Hiltons had a home again. Six
days later, though, off went the team on another long road
trip.

That very morning at eight, we shared a sight familiar

to all of us: players and wives and girlfriends hanging out in the parking lot saying our goodbyes, watching the guys, each responsible for his own equipment, loading the bus.

Hard as it was for Dana to say goodbye to Stan, the saddest goodbye that morning was the one being said by Claudio and Kim Carasco. Claudio, who plays second base, is from the Dominican Republic and Kim's from Iowa. They met several seasons ago while Claudio was playing in Class A at Waterloo in the Midwest League. They had married in Iowa and had a handsome three-year-old son, Tavis. Kim was hugging Claudio, tears in her eyes, because her second baby was due "any time." It tore me up knowing what Kim was feeling, her husband leaving town with the team and her family in Iowa. Mike, who is never comfortable with teary situations, tried to lighten the mood when he yelled at us while boarding the bus: "Cross your legs, Kim, we'll be home in six days."

She did. It didn't work. Two days later I received a call at 9 A.M. (thank God). Kim thought she was in labor. She arrived at my apartment three hours later. Tavis and Shannon Carlson were with her. Shannon was the girlfriend of the newest member of the team, Chris Isaacson.

By three o'clock we were headed for the hospital. I was the D.H. (Designated Handholder), an improvised replacement for Claudio. Maybe Kim didn't feel all that comfortable with me—the low-fuel light was on all the way to the hospital. With Claudio on hold in his Burlington, Vermont, hotel room five hours away and her folks in Iowa, Shannon and I knew we would be "family" for the duration. Kim did super. Three hours later, just after 6 P.M., Friday, July 1, 1988, Kim presented Claudio their first baby daughter—via long distance.

By the time Tiahni was an hour old, she had been visited by nearly every wife on the club. The nurse came in to take Tiahni to the nursery, since she had not even been weighed or measured. But she took the tiny bundle out of the incubator long enough to allow her mom a quick squeeze. Kim began to cry as she looked at her baby, so fresh from God, in her arms. Hers were not the only tears in the room.

The most important event of our summer had just taken place. Where the Williamsport Bills finished in the standings, which of our players were invited to Instructional, pale in comparison. The experience we had shared may not be duplicated for any of us however long we are in baseball. Outside the game, maybe it can't be.

We wives of summer had responded to what could have been a dismal experience and helped make it one of the best of our lives.

How can you stand being in the minors after having been so long in the majors? That question—sometimes implied —is posed to me almost every day. Since last July 1, I tell the Kim Carasco story to anyone who will listen.

Do Mike and I still have goals after all the years in ball? Mike never got the Mercedes Brad Corbett once offered him. And he has never worn a World Series ring.

A few weeks ago I saw a chart in *U.S.A. Today* that listed the oldest managers in major leagues. Los Angeles's Tom LaSorda, at sixty-one, headed the list. Could Mike, thirty-nine, manage another twenty-two years?

What counts is how long he continues to love the game. I see no end to that.

But the survey spoke to me, too: *Sharon Hargrove, you may have at least twenty more years in this game.*

To that I say: *Praise the Lord!*

Until next season.

Appendix: Smelling the Roses

16445 North 63rd Drive
Glendale, AZ 85306
November 6, 1987

Dear Sharon,

Thanks for your kind letter of Oct. 27 and continued interest in my thoughts. Maybe with our "Series share" we can get a typewriter, but in the meantime please bear with my handwriting.

To answer your question [Has being in the World Series changed our outlook?], I have to explain everything this year has been for us. You have to go back to spring training.

For some reason I had a feeling this would be a year of great things for Steve. Courting thoughts of success is pretty foreign to me so it felt unusual.

Steve had an excellent spring, was among the top 10 in both leagues in batting average. Then the other shoe fell. The Tony Pena trade. O.K., so we're back to Sunday starts. Steve had hoped he had proven he was good enough to platoon on the Cardinals with lefthanded hitting Mike La-Valliere. Then Tony Pena's injury. Steve does great again. Maybe there's something to these feelings. Then back to Sundays. It was like a roller coaster—the thrills of the drops and curves but then the ride would slow and stop. It was hard to let the highs go and face reality. For Steve, it was so much fun to be "part" of the team in playing and winning.

Amazingly enough, however, just when Steve felt his hard work had gone for nothing, he'd get to play and contribute. It would feel good again.

Meanwhile, I had my first opportunity to be a part of it all. Some close friendships were made. We did some charity work and even had the opportunity to do some "Cardinal Wives" radio shows. It was *so* gratifying to be out there supporting Steve as more than window dressing in the stands.

To have won the National League East title was satisfying. To beat the Giants was magical. To see Steve play in the Series was pure joy. To have the years of struggle come to this was indescribable. A TV station played "[I had the] Time of My Life" while clips of the Series played in slow motion. I think that's how I'll remember it: Slow moving pictures. . . .

Minneapolis: the intimidating "Dome," whistles, hankies, the World Series logo painted on the turf, the banners and signs, just taking it all in.

Back to Busch: hope against hope, 50,000 fans in red, the Clydesdales, Ozzie's flip, twirling towels, fireworks in victory for 3 straight nights. Can we take one more game? Can I find 2 more outfits to wear?

Minneapolis again: fans more hostile now gloating after Game 6. Magrane throwing tomorrow—not much success in post-season play. Can Danny [Cox] do it again?

I'm at the ball park at 6:15 for Game 7. Cards' lineup flashing on the board: *hitting 8th, #25.* Are you serious? *Game 7 of the World Series?* Shock, since he hasn't started in post-season play. Then reality hits. *Oh great, no pressure.*

I fight back tears of pride because I know what this means to Steve. My heart's racing. A nervous wreck. Karen Dawley, my best friend on the team, puts her arm around me and says, "He'll do fine. So calm down."

Now come the time to pray: "Please God if ever there was a day to be 'on' let it be this one, and whoever wins, thanks for this day." I prayed for courage, wisdom and accuracy in that order. My prayers were answered and then some that night. Steve really shone despite the loss. Somehow the old adage rang true that things happen for a reason. Maybe the ups and downs of our years in baseball had to occur in order to make this day so special.

It's like your wedding day or the day your kids were born. It'll never happen again in the same way, but the memories will stay vivid and become more precious as time passes. With the plays at the plate, especially the "Gaetti Crunch," I knew if Steve had a chance he wouldn't fold. That's the kind of catcher he is. His animation over his teammates' good plays and his frustration when the Twins' winning run scored are equal evidence of his makeup.

It was a disappointment to have gone so far and not gone all the way. The Twins' time had come. When Day One of spring training arrives, we're all back in last place.

Steve's final thoughts as he closed his eyes for the night: "Now my kids can say their dad played in a World Series."

Sincerely,
Patti Lake

Index

Index

Index

Index

Index

Index

Safe at Home was composed into type on a Compugraphic digital phototypesetter in ten point Trump Medieval with three points of spacing between the lines. Trump Italic was selected for display. The book was designed by Cameron Poulter, typeset by Metricomp, Inc., printed offset by Thomson-Shore, Inc., and bound by John H. Dekker & Sons. The paper on which the book is printed is designed for an effective life of at least three hundred years.

Texas A&M University Press : College Station